EXPERIMENTAL
PHENOMENOLOGY

Books by Don Ihde

EXPERIMENTAL PHENOMENOLOGY
LISTENING AND VOICE
PHENOMENOLOGY AND EXISTENTIALISM *(with Richard Zaner, eds.)*
SENSE AND SIGNIFICANCE
HERMENEUTIC PHENOMENOLOGY
EXISTENTIAL TECHNICS
HERMENEUTICS AND DECONSTRUCTION *(with Hugh Silverman, eds.)*
DESCRIPTIONS *(with Hugh Silverman, eds.)*
CONSEQUENCES OF PHENOMENOLOGY

EXPERIMENTAL PHENOMENOLOGY

An Introduction

DON IHDE

State University of New York Press

First published by The Putnam Publishing Group.

Published by
State University of New York Press, Albany

For information, address State University of New York Press,
90 State Street, Suite 700, Albany NY 12207

Library of Congress Cataloging in Publication Data

Ihde, Don, 1934-
  Experimental phenomenology.

  Reprint. Originally published: New York : Putnam,
1977.
  Includes bibliographical references and index.
  1. Phenomenology.   I. Title.
[B829.5.I33 1986]   142'.7   85-27768
ISBN 0-88706-198-2
ISBN 0-88706-199-0 (pbk.)

10 9 8 7 6 5

ACKNOWLEDGMENTS

Drawings of the Necker Cube, Projections of a Cube and of a Depth Reversal of a Real Object are from "Multistability in Perception" by Fred Attneave. Copyright © (December 1971) by Scientific American, Inc. Reprinted with permission, all rights reserved.

Imagining: A Phenomenological Study by Edward S. Casey. Copyright © 1976 by Indiana University Press. Reprinted by permission of the publisher.

The Social Construction of Reality: A Treatise in the Sociology of Knowledge by Peter L. Berger and Thomas Luckmann. Copyright © 1966 by Peter L. Berger and Thomas Luckmann. Reprinted by permission of Doubleday and Company, Inc.

"The Experience of Technology: A Phenomenology of Human-Machine Relations" by Don Ihde. Copyright © 1974 *Cultural Hermeneutics*. Reprinted by permission of the author.

Preface

Like so many philosophical ventures, this book began accidentally. I had just read an article on multi-stable perception, which had been pointed out to me by a colleague who knew I had been doing some hesitating and preliminary work on ambiguous drawings such as those employed by Maurice Merleau-Ponty and Ludwig Wittgenstein. I thought the article inadequate and sometimes inaccurate. Because I contemplated making a reply to it, I took the issues raised to my phenomenology classes, playing with them and trying out ideas with my students. The result was a happy surprise: the students were able to grasp certain essential ideas in phenomenology through the use of visual examples much more quickly than with any previous approach.

It also became apparent that the students needed a concrete introduction to phenomenology—that is, one that works through examples in a step-by-step fashion without being either boring or too difficult. Thus was born *EXPERIMENTAL PHENOMENOLOGY.*

The expert in the field will here recognize a Husserlian flavor to this introduction. This is deliberate; while my own sympathies do not ultimately lie with Husserl, I am convinced that phenomenology must begin with his approach, which is more like analytic philosophy than other types of phenomenology. First come rigor and distinction-making; then come depth and extrapolation.

I would like to thank a much larger number of persons than I can mention here, first among them, Patrick Heelan, whose stimulating conversation first encouraged me to write on this topic. I would like also to acknowledge the helpful criticisms of my students and colleagues at Stony Brook, the typing and preparation of the manuscript by Lillian Richardson, and the helpful editing and grammatical revision provided by Robin Elliser and Margaret Thomas. I am also continually grateful to my wife and children for their patience and understanding: when writing, I am inclined to be "somewhere else" during conversation or dinner. They, too, have had some share in developing the text. Several of the most imaginative hermeneutic stories were inventions of my children who, better than many older persons, are often able to grasp an essential insight with ease.

Table of Contents

Preface   **7**

Chapter One
             Introduction: Doing Phenomenology   **13**

Chapter Two
             Indians and the Elephant: **29**
             Phenomena and the
             Phenomenological Reductions

Chapter Three
             The Visual Field: First   **55**
             Phenomenological Excursus

Chapter Four
             Illusions and Multi-Stable Phenomena: **67**
             A Phenomenological Deconstruction

Chapter Five
             Variations upon Deconstruction: **81**
             Possibilities and Topography

Chapter Six

Expanded Variations and   91
Phenomenological Reconstruction

Chapter Seven

Horizons: Adequacy and Invariance   109

Chapter Eight

Projection: Expanding   123
Phenomenology

Chapter Nine

Interdisciplinary Phenomenology   135

Epilogue   152

                                         155
Index of Names

For my students (and teachers)

Chapter One

Introduction:
Doing Phenomenology

Many disciplines are better learned by entering into the doing than by mere abstract study. This is often the case with the most abstract as well as the seemingly more practical disciplines. For example, within the philosophical disciplines, logic must be learned through the use of examples and actual problem solving. Only after some time and struggle does the student begin to develop the insights and intuitions that enable him to see the centrality and relevance of this mode of thinking. This learning by doing is essential in many of the sciences. The laboratory provides the context within which one learns to see according to a scientific modality. Gradually the messy blob of frog's innards begins to take the recognizable shape of well-defined organs, blood vessels and the like. Similarly, only after a good deal of observation do the sparks in the bubble chamber become recognizable as the specific movements of identifiable particles.

In philosophy also, this learning by example and experience is an important element—but learning by doing is more important in some types of philosophy than in other types. For example, in the two dominant contemporary styles of philosophy, analytic and phenomenological, doing either an analysis or a description calls for putting into practice a certain method of inquiry. But in the case of phenomenology, I would make an even stronger claim: *Without doing phenomenology, it may be practically impossible to understand phenomenology.* This is not to say that one may not learn *about* phenomenology by other means. Certainly, much can be learned about the history, the structure of the inquiry, the methodological presuppositions of phenomenology (or any type of philosophy) by a careful reading of major thinkers, secondary writers and criticism. In fact, learning the background and establishing the context is not only usual for learning a philosophical style, it is an essential element of a comprehensive grasp of the discipline. Nevertheless, without entering into the *doing*, the basic thrust and import of phenomenology is likely to be misunderstood at the least or missed at most. Phenomenology, in the first instance, is like an investigative science, an essential component of which is experiment. Phenomenology is *experimental* and its experiments are conducted according to a carefully worked out set of controls and methods. It is this dimension of phenomenology that this book addresses. The thought-experiments—or better, experience-experiments—that are worked out here are attempts to show the way in which phenomenological inquiry proceeds.

Most academic settings have ample resources for supplementary reading in the form of primary texts, anthologies and interpretations.[1] I would recommend particularly readings in the works of Edmund Husserl, Martin Heidegger and Maurice Merleau-Ponty.[2] The difficulty with these texts is that they present the beginner with accomplished results, often in a language that is, at first, quite difficult to penetrate. Such books are not self-explanatory. They often presuppose a good deal of philosophical sophistication in general and some minimal familiarity with at least one particular tradition within philosophy (the transcendental tradition). Moreover, even with this background, the originators of the phenomenological style of philosophy themselves had a difficulty in moving from purely textual acquaintance with phenomenology to its import as a means of investigation. Martin Heidegger (clearly one of the giants of the phenomenological movement) confessed that although he had thoroughly read the main works of Edmund Husserl (the primary "inventor" of phenomenology), he was not able to understand the full sense of phenomenology until he learned to "see phenomenologically."

> . . . My repeated beginning also remained unsatisfactory, because I couldn't get over a main difficulty. It concerned the simple question how thinking's manner of procedure which called itself "phenomenology" was to be carried out. . . . My perplexity decreased slowly, my confusion dissolved laboriously, only after I met Husserl personally in his workshop. . . . Husserl's teaching took place in a step-bystep training in phenomenological "seeing" which at the same time demanded that one relinquish the untested use of philosophical knowledge. . . . I myself practiced phenomenological seeing, teaching and learning in Husserl's proximity after 1919.[3]

This has been a common experience of those who have learned to do and appreciate phenomenology.

This book aims to overcome some of the difficulties attendant on first learning phenomenology by stressing from the outset the doing, the actual practice of a phenomenological descriptive analysis. The methods of phenomenology will be shown by way of undertaking a special set of inquiries. Phenomenology is to be taught here by way of experiment. But at the same time, it is my hope that the reader will grasp some of the excitement and implication of phenomenology for philosophy and other disciplines.

Of course, no inquiry begins in a vacuum. Even a relatively unfamiliar method or type of thought must make at least minimal contact with previous or extant thought. This is no less the case with phenomenology than it is with every other type of philosophy. To establish the context, this chapter first addresses the present state of affairs. Phenomenology as a term is currently in the air. One hears it, not only in philosophy, but also with respect to other disciplines. There is (or was) a "phenomenological physics," which has as one of its elements a return to a close look at certain phenomena specifically considered in isolation from current or dominant theories of explanation. There is talk about a "phenomenological psychology" or at least about phenomenological elements in psychology. In this so-called phenomenology, the "subjective experiences" of a subject are made thematic. In the social sciences, current ethnomethodology and the notion of "participant observation" have links to the phenomenological tradition. There is also a "phenomenology of religion," the beginnings of a "phenomenological" literary criticism, a revival of interest in the phenomenological dimensions of logic, and a host of other new, but as yet undeveloped incursions of phenomenology into other disciplines.

Initially, the current spread of the term phenomenology, and the jargon or tribal language that accompanies it, is not necessarily helpful. Mere familiarity with terms often leads to a false sense of security gained from a superficial understanding of their meaning; this superficial understanding floats on the surface of a mind cluttered with the debris of misunderstandings and criticisms arising from these misunderstandings. On the other hand, it is now clearly the case that within philosophy, phenomenology is recognized as a major style of philosophical inquiry. This stands in marked contrast to the philosophical scene only a decade ago. Today most major departments have at least one philosopher who specializes in some version of scholarship directed towards phenomenology, whether as an active proponent, a critic, or a highly interested onlooker. As time goes on, more and more departments are developing subspecialities in phenomenology.

Precisely because phenomenology is still a minority voice of current American philosophy (though it is no longer totally unknown or merely a target of severe criticism), it cannot claim "self-evidence" or have common assumptions regarding, even its own, knowledge of itself.

A few preliminary glances both at claims made by phenomenologists and at familiar criticisms facing phenomenology, may clarify the context in which an introduction to the subject may properly begin. In what follows, I shall pair claims made by phenomenologists with familiar and widespread criticisms of phenomenology, trying to show, both why certain preliminary criticisms are all but unavoidable and why much of this criticism is not necessarily well-founded. Finally, however, each reader must see for himself or herself, but I hope that judgment will be informed by direct knowledge.

First, phenomenology as a relatively new philosophical method claims to be a *radical* way of thought. Its founder, Edmund Husserl, claimed, "There is only one *radical* self investigation, and it is phenomenological."[4] Martin Heidegger, following Husserl, claimed, "Phenomenology is our way of access to what is to be the theme of ontology, and it is our way of giving it demonstrative precision. *Only as phenomenology, is ontology possible.*"[5] Clearly these are strong claims and ultimately their fulfillment must come only through what may actually be delivered via phenomenology.

But as a radical philosophy, phenomenology necessarily departs from familiar ways of doing things and accepted ways of thinking. It overturns many presuppositions ordinarily taken for granted and seeks to establish a new perspective from which to view things. Whether or not it succeeds in this task, remains to be seen, but note what must necessarily be the case if phenomenology *is* a radical philosophy, quite apart from its success or failure.

If a method is genuinely radical and new, then its new concepts and methods will in some degree be unfamiliar and strange—at least at first. The very displacement of the familiar is such that an initial obscurity will result. A new language will flow from the new concepts, or at the very least, new meanings will be given to older terms. In any case, mastery of a particular language will be called for if the philosophy is to be understood. I shall call this "essential obscurity" and shall try to show that such "essential obscurity" is temporary. It belongs to a certain stage of learning.

In a negative form, this characterization of phenomenology is a familiar criticism. It is widely held that phenomenology is obscure and difficult, if not impossible to understand. Here, the reasons for possible obscurity must be clarified. If, at base, phenomenology should turn out to be contradictory within itself; if its fundamental concepts are confused *after* being scrutinized; or if its claims, not on an initial look but after critical examination, are ill-founded; then the criticism is well-founded. But if the criticisms are superficial, the result of insufficient insight or understanding, then the issue is quite different. It is with this possibility in mind that I would like to examine several distinct forms of confusion.

I have already noted that there is an initial "essential obscurity," which necessarily belongs to the first stage of phenomenology. But this type of obscurity may be temporary as well as not unique to phenomenology. It is rather the type of obscurity that comes with any genuinely new mode of inquiry. Historically, one may point to many such examples in relation to the history of science. Revolutions in science have been characterized by Thomas Kuhn as "paradigm shifts."[6] These occurrences are shifts in the way things are viewed. Until the view is re-settled, until the basis for the new perspective is solidified, there remains an area of possible misunderstanding between those holding to the former paradigm and those holding to the new paradigm; frequently, there may be problems for those within the new paradigm until its lines of sight are sufficiently freed from the past paradigm. It is this genesis of shift and clarification that belongs to what I have called "essential obscurity."

For instance, when Copernicus began to develop his theory of a heliocentric universe in which the sun was the center of the planetary system, most scholars of his time thought such a notion odd, obscure and even unthinkable. It was a counter-intuitive idea in the sense that, what one saw with one's own eyes and what one knew by established theory was the centrality of the earth. The sun rose and set in an observed movement from a fixed earth which one could experience. These facts were grounded in long-held theories. What was lacking, for our purposes here, was a requisite question: "from what perspective and in what framework can such a departure from common sense become possible?" Copernicus had already projected a new, as yet only imaginary, stance, different from man's ordinary position on the earth. He became as a distant deity watching the earth move around the sun from a position that he, as an earthbound man, had never inhabited nor could have inhabited at that time. To see the glory of the earth from afar has become possible only in our own time—but its abstract possibility was already latent in the revolution of standpoint contained in Copernicus' theory.

Given this shift, what counted as fact was seen differently by those who took the earthbound stance as primary and those who joined the Copernican revolution with its heavenly stance. Thus argument could no longer presume the same grounds.

This new stance opened the way for even further extrapolation, which Copernicus, himself, found difficult to accept. Giordano Bruno, for example, soon made the extrapolation that if a displacement of the earth from its center made a new view possible, it was also possible to displace the sun as well. To leap outwards was but a first step; if our solar system could be so viewed, why could not the other stars also be so viewed, and so on infinitely. Thus the postulation of other planetary systems, multiple suns and even multiple inhabited worlds in an infinite universe could be posited. The first revolution, which destroyed the earthbound stance, now could be extrapolated to a possible infinity of positions, all equally possible.

Historically, we know that, in spite of resistance, argument and even persecution, what was previously taken as odd, obscure and unthinkable became accepted, even taken for granted or obvious as we might say now. It was this struggle for the requisite insight which would make things clear from a wholly new standpoint that created the first "essential obscurity." This obscurity in turn became "intuitive" and could later be seen as a temporary obscurity.

The implicit claim here is that, if phenomenology is indeed a new modality of thought, the source of its obscurity is only a temporary or "essential obscurity," which necessarily belongs to the new. Once the point of view that makes its view of things possible is made clear, its language and meaning yield their own clarity.

But there is a second and somewhat more superficial obscurity which can accompany the first. This obscurity is the initial obscurity that accompanies all theoretical and technical disciplines. When one first learns a discipline, one also must learn a "tribal language." In philosophy, those who read Kant for the first time, or Leibniz, or even Nietzsche, may find words being used in a different and often technical way. Philosophy rarely reads like fiction, and at first, many people have to read texts phrase by phrase in order to comprehend them. One first approximates the internal meaning or, as Merleau-Ponty points out, one "sings" the language before one clearly understands it.[7] This type of obscurity is also temporary; it calls only for a serious attempt at entering the new language. Phenomenology's tribal language contains a whole vocabulary of technical terms: "intentionality," "*epoché*," "the phenomenological reductions," "being-in-the-world" and the like, while quite familiar to the tribe of phenomenologists, remain opaque to the other tribes of the world. But if a discipline is to be mastered, the technical language simply must be learned. That is as true of sciences, logic, alternate styles of philosophy as it is of phenomenology.

A third kind of obscurity sometimes occurs which is to be deplored. Essentially, this consists of the language some phenomenologists, particularly commentators and imitators, introduce by inserting unnecessary obscurity and even cuteness into their language. Whatever the motive, any attempt to cover confusion or pretend profundity by means of excess verbiage is naturally distasteful.

Finally, there is the possibility of a *fundamental* obscurity. Such an obscurity reveals fundamental inconsistency, confusion or a final lack of plausibility. This obscurity can be discovered *only* by careful analysis and rarely appears on the surface. In philosophical history, such deep obscurity has nearly always been discovered only after great effort and time, usually by surpassing the philosophy being criticized. But surpassing a philosophy entails learning its lessons, and so, no revolution in thought is total.

Thus, the claim here is not that phenomenology will be shown to be without possible flaw or limitation. The claim is, rather, that most presumed obscurity will be shown to be of the temporary variety; once its stance is properly appreciated, its own clarity can and will emerge.

The second claim made by phenomenologists is that at its first stage, phenomenology has developed a genuine "science of experi-ence," which Husserl earlier called a rigorous "descriptive psy-chology." This *phenomenological* psychology is quite different from most extant psychologies, as I shall attempt to show in the body of this book, although the examples are limited primarily to perceptual examples.

Paired with this second claim is a widespread objection to phe-nomenology which takes the form of accusing phenomenology of being "subjectivistic" and, at its extreme, accuses it of being a re-version to 19th century introspective psychology. Critics of this per-suasion intimate that this subjectivity is bad and unworthy both of philosophy, which must be distinct from psychology, and of psy-chology, which in much of its current phase avoids the question of so-called subjective states. Everyone, of course, would not consider the examination of experience or introspection to be bad. But the question is not really whether phenomenology examines experience, but *how* it does, and with what method and result.

That phenomenology claims to have developed a genuine "science of experience" despite the objections of those who are suspicious of subjectivity calls for a prolonged examination of what phenomenology studies and how phenomenology interprets experi-ence. In terms of its earlier development, phenomenology claims to examine human experience and to be a rigorous science of experi-ence. This inextricably involves psychological questions.

However, confused with the issue concerning psychology is an is-sue of strictly philosophical import concerning theories of evidence. At stake is a radically different framework within which the ques-tion of what shall count as evidence takes its place. As a prelimi-nary, it can be stated that phenomenology demands that its evidence must be "intuitable," which means, in its proper context, that what is given or accepted as evidence must be actually experienceable within the limits of and related to the human experiencer. But, as will be shown later, this notion is a highly complex one and must be qualified to such an extent that what is ordinarily taken as experi-ence itself undergoes significant change.

Precisely because phenomenology directs its first glance upon experience, it necessarily employs some form of reflection, and in part this reflection must include what has heretofore been known as introspective data. However, there are serious misunderstandings of what has been meant by introspection, particularly as it is transformed in a phenomenological account. Yet, insofar as so-called introspective data are relevant to a comprehensive account of experience, they must be included. What cannot be admitted is that introspection is *the* method of phenomenology.

The confusion between what shall count as psychology and what shall count as philosophy arose at the beginning of phenomenology, and in part must be attributed to the language employed by Edmund Husserl. Husserl's use of language made such objections all but inevitable. The terms "ego," "consciousness," "subjective states" and "transcendental subjectivity" cannot help but lead the casual reader to the conclusion that phenomenology is a type of psychology. What the casual reader misses is the transformation of meaning that occurs in terms within phenomenology from Husserl on.

This linguistic confusion belongs to the general problem of introducing a new mode of thought within an already known language, in this case, the language of modern philosophy with its notion of "subject" and "object." For a new thought to be expressed, it must either introduce a radically new language—at the risk of not being understood at all—or stretch the meanings of previous terms to cover new uses. In its history phenomenology has done both, but for the most part Husserl took already well-used terms and gave them special meanings. The result, however, is that one must read carefully and critically to detect the new meanings he sought to establish, meanings often contrary to the traditional ones. Compounding this situation, Husserl's published works lack carefully worked out concrete examples that would have clarified this heuristic use of language.

To counter the accusation of subjectivism, phenomenologists have tried to draw a sharp line between what has ordinarily been known as introspection and what is developed phenomenologically as "reflexivity." Although the distinction will be developed more thoroughly in subsequent chapters, it is important initially to note that introspection is, roughly speaking, the straightforward taking of subjective data, usually interpreted as "directly present to the mind." This notion of direct presence belongs to both the rationalist and empiricist traditions in philosophy and finds its theoretical context in what phenomenologists call Cartesianism. These traditions locate subjective phenomena "within" a subject and contrast these phenomena with objective phenomena located "outside" the subject. Furthermore, it was Modern Philosophy that brought into fullest and sharpest usage the terms "subject," "ego," "material bodies," etc.—the very language that Husserl at first adopted.

Initially, phenomenology transforms the Modern tradition by taking two steps. First, what was previously regarded as "present to the mind" is taken within phenomenology as a genuine field of possible data: phenomena. This field, however, needs to be fully discriminated and clarified; that task constitutes one part of phenomenological inquiry. This being so, all phenomena as "present to a subject" may be regarded as worthy of investigation. Images, percepts, moods, arithmetical phenomena or whatever, may be a valid region for inquiry. It is in this sense, and in this sense only, that so-called introspective data may be considered. But it should also be pointed out that *extrospective* data are equally to be considered. What is investigated, is the field of phenomena.

But within phenomenology, phenomena are never taken as self-evident nor are they inevitably interpreted as "within the mind." Both introspective and extrospective phenomena must be located more precisely within the phenomenological analysis, and it is at this point that the distinction between "introspection" and "reflexivity" comes into play. For phenomenology, the central feature of experience is a *structure* called "intentionality," which correlates all things experienced with the mode of experience to which the experience is referred. The full meaning of this notion will be explained at length in the next chapter. Here, it is only important to note that, far from being self-evident or initially transparent, the "subject" is enigmatic for phenomenology. It is known only *reflexively* from which phenomena and how these phenomena are made present to it. "Introspection," in its Cartesian sense, is taken by phenomenologists to be a naive notion open to the same degree of suspicion in which subjectivism is held. But at the same time, phenomenology does not simply revert to a reductionistic strategy which discards phenomena together with the problems concerning access to phenomena.

In order to set the context, I have taken two initial claims of phenomenologists and paired them with two widespread objections to phenomenology. It should now be apparent that another preliminary task is to introduce at least a minimal vocabulary and set of concepts so that the experiments can get underway. This book will proceed by establishing certain elementary phenomenological distinctions and terms, putting these in as clear a fashion as possible by means of concrete demonstrated examples.

What an elementary—though not to say easy—introduction to phenomenology must accomplish, if it is to be successful, is a restatement of the main themes, ideas and directions of a style of thought in a language that has been given a clear and illustrated rationale. Simplicity, here, will mean a step-by-step procedure with particular regard to the main terms and concepts of phenomenology. I will introduce the basic vocabulary of the tribal language, but will often put explanations in my own language in order to show the basic sense of the phenomenological method.

Simplicity will require following a process of investigation, since this book is intended as an introduction to phenomenology through experiments. Through the examination of concrete problems as opposed to merely programmatic texts, experimental phenomenology attempts to show *how* phenomenology works. Because this method makes an extra demand upon the reader, it is essential that the reading of this text be accompanied by following actual experiential examples. While the language of the text will be as clear and simple as possible, the demand upon the reader will be more complex. He must *see* what is going on, and by that I mean *see* in its most concrete and literal sense.

The method I will use arises out of an actual set of phenomenological investigations that have been conducted over the last few years in relation to certain problems and puzzles concerning visual perception. Although I shall employ examples involving the other senses, the core examples are taken from a set of familiar, traditional and already much-interpreted visual illusions, reversible figures and so-called multi-stable visual objects.

The choice of this set of examples, which will be reinterpreted in phenomenological terms, itself exemplifies one tactic of phenomenological investigation. The use of simple, familiar examples deliberately opens the way to the sense of phenomenology through an "experiential given" (given in the sense of intuitively familiar). For what could be more familiar than these psychological illustrations? They even appear on restaurant placemats as puzzles in which lines which "appear" curved are in "reality" straight, and as two-dimensional cubes that spontaneously reverse themselves before one's eyes. Moreover, visual as opposed to other sensory examples are implicitly taken to be paradigm examples for all perception and knowledge.[8] Seeing is clear and distinct and is the external counterpart to the internal sense of reason which is *insight*. Finally, these puzzles and illustrations have already been well interpreted by the standard psychologies and the results, for a "naive" observer, are well-known and predictable.

My task will be to take a new look at these examples and try to see and to show them in a phenomenological framework. While doing this, I shall attempt to show how and why phenomenology works the way it does. I hope, that in this process, some of the radicalism of phenomenology will begin to show itself, so that the beginner not only will be interested in what is going on, but will also probe into further relations and implications for his own discipline. Secondarily, I hope that some of the prejudices and misunderstandings about phenomenology will either be eliminated or compensated for in a more lucid manner. It is my contention that in its essence, phenomenology is neither obscure nor esoteric and that it holds important implications for a whole range of disciplines.

For the serious student of philosophy, I hope that an introduction by way of phenomenological experimentation will kindle a small sense of excitement for a style of philosophy that does not leave things the way they are, but seeks to make discoveries of its own. A phenomenolgical analysis (or description, as it is technically called) is more than mere analysis. It is a probing for what is genuinely discoverable and potentially there, but not often seen. Phenomenology is the door to the possible, a possible that can be experienced and verified through the procedures which are, in fact, the stuff of experimental phenomenology.

Notes

1. For an anthology consisting of the primary authors on the central themes of phenomenology, see Richard M. Zaner and Don Ihde, *Phenomenology and Existentialism* (New York: Capricorn Books, 1973).

2. The three most important works to be cited are: Edmund Husserl, *Ideas: General Introduction to Pure Phenomenology*; Martin Heidegger, *Being and Time*; and Maurice Merleau-Ponty, *Phenomenology of Perception*.

3. Martin Heidegger, *On Time and Being*, translated by Joan Stambaugh (New York: Harper and Row, 1972), pp. 76, 78.

4. Edmund Husserl, *Cartesian Meditations*, translated by Dorion Cairns (The Hague: Martinus Nijhoff, 1960), p. 153.

5. Martin Heidegger, *Being and Time*, translated by John Macquarrie and Edward Robinson (New York: Harper and Row, 1962), p. 60.

6. Thomas Kuhn, *The Structure of Scientific Revolutions* (Chicago: University of Chicago Press, 1962).

7. Maurice Merleau-Ponty, *Phenomenology of Perception*, translated by Colin Smith (London: Routledge and Kegan Paul, 1962), pp. 179, 187.

8. For a phenomenological account of auditory experience in contrast, see Don Ihde, *Listening and Voice: A Phenomenology of Sound* (Athens: Ohio University Press, 1976).

Chapter Two

Indians and the Elephant:
Phenomena and the Phenomenological
Reductions

To get off the ground, a philosophy must choose that with which it begins. At the same time, if it is ultimately to claim to be comprehensive, this choice must be one that potentially includes all that may be needed for universality. Phenomenology, tautologically the study of phenomena, makes this claim as well. The maxim Edmund Husserl coined to characterize phenomenology was, "To the things themselves!"[1] Martin Heidegger, elaborating upon this maxim, noted, ". . . the expression '*phenomena*' signifies *that which shows itself in itself*, the manifest."[2] And, echoing Husserl's call for radicalism in thought, he continued, "Thus the term 'phenomenology' expresses a maxim which can be formulated as 'To the things themselves!' It is opposed to all free-floating constructions and accidental findings; it is opposed to those pseudoproblems that parade themselves as 'problems', often for generations at a time."[3] But the question is "how do we properly get to the phenomena themselves?" There is a circle here, which may first be posed in Augus-

29

tinian fashion: In order to find out, I must in some sense already know; but in order to know, I must find out.

Perhaps a hoary fable can set the tone. Recall the fable of the blind Indians and the elephant, in which a number of feelers-of-elephants were given the task of deciding what the elephant "really" is. The first blind man felt the tail of the beast and related that the elephant was really like a snake, long and sinuous; the second, felt the elephant's leg and related that the elephant was really like a tree trunk, rough and sturdy, etc.

I suppose the fable is meant to make the valid point that parts should not be taken for the whole—but judged by phenomenological standards, these particular blind men are worse off than that. In the first place, in spite of their limited access to the "phenomenon-elephant," the blind men do have "the thing itself" before them. But yet from the outset they miss what may be gained. They do not examine even the limited experience they have with sufficient precision or depth. To feel the hairy, coarse and knotty-boned tail of the elephant is very unlike grasping the smooth, scaly and not slimy body of a snake. Nor is the horizontally folded and relatively pliable leg skin of the elephant much like the usually vertically lined and rigid bark of a tree. From the outset, their descriptions are sloppy and based primarily upon simile and traditional beliefs rather than upon a careful analysis of the *phenomenon* before them.

Secondly, they show a tendency typical of an easy or fast "philosophy," that is, they choose to define the reality of the elephant far too quickly, not only prior to examining the whole, but even prior to a careful descriptive analysis of its parts. Leaping to a premature definition prevents the fullness of the "phenomenon-elephant" from being discovered. Instead, it is masked by superficiality.

From the fable, and more particularly, from the partial phenomenological critique of the fable, it can be seen that a certain initial weighting occurs in phenomenology. This has been characterized as radically empirical, at least in the sense that what is first dealt with is what is taken to be the experience. Such a radically empirical beginning, while not lacking a definitional dimension, stands in contrast to other initial choices of theory, for example, an axiomatic-constructive theory.

An axiomatic-constructive theory begins with a series of definitions and formal relations prior to investigation. Formal systems such as mathematics, logic and some theoretical sciences begin with a preset language and set of definitions. In such systems, clarity is a function of the definition, and what is "intuitive" refers to logical transparency. A system that begins thus must pay a price for its choice. Often the price is that, that which is not stipulated may not fall within the definition. This excludes certain phenomena on the one hand, while on the other, phenomena within the definition may be left hanging abstractly as it were, merely contained.

In contrast, phenomenology begins with a kind of empirical observation directed at the whole field of possible experiential phenomena. Initially, it attempts to see things in a particularly open way that is analogous to Copernicus' *new* vision of the universe. Ideally, this stance tries to create an *opening* of a particular type towards things; it wishes to recapture the original sense of wonder which Aristotle claimed was the originating motive for philosophy. Thus, its first methodological moves seek to circumvent certain kinds of predefinition.

A price must be paid for this choice: definitions, if arrived at at all, come quite late, subjecting the initial language of phenomenology to later revision and change as the inquiry progresses. Its benefit is that this initial openness allows the field of inquiry to be wide and relatively free of structure. Such a beginning may appear paradoxical. The paradox consists in the fact that without some—at least general—idea of what and how one is to look at a thing, how can anything be seen? Yet, if what is to be seen is to be seen without prejudice or preconception, how can it be circumscribed by definition? This is one way of stating what is known in phenomenology as a hermeneutic circle, but which I shall call here a *dialectic of interpretation*.

This dialectic of interpretation generates a distance between the axiomatic and the observational in such a way that a direction of inquiry may be taken. The direction first taken is towards the "things themselves," that is, the phenomena present to experience. In this respect, what I shall call the observational side gets a primary weight. Careful looking precedes classification and systematization, and systematization and classification are made to follow what the phenomenon shows.

I want to emphasize, however, that this is an initial weighting and direction, a beginning—not an end, although the beginning determines how any end is to be achieved. A genuinely radical empiricism may, after all, find that things are not at all as they first seemed. This weighting which demands that we first look carefully at what is experienced, and how it is experienced, must be more precisely specified. In what follows, I have for the most part made a somewhat simplified adaptation of Husserlian language and methodology.

The first steps of phenomenological looking are usually called an *epoché*, which means to suspend or step back from our ordinary ways of looking, to set aside our usual assumptions regarding things. Within this general stance, particular levels of stepping back are then determined; these levels are termed *phenomenological reductions*. I shall interpret these specifications as working rules or directions for the way the investigation may proceed. Thus *epoché* and *phenomenological reductions* may also be called *hermeneutic rules*, since they provide the shape or focus of the inquiry. Hermeneutic in its broadest sense means interpretation, and rules give shape to an interpretation.

The first question is directed to the region of inquiry. What are we to investigate? The motto "to the things themselves" indicates an infinitely open field, including all and any phenomena whatsoever— but only as they are given to experience. Our attention to things that are *given* to experience is with the proviso that we attend to them only as given. This means that we can attend to all the usual furniture of experience, including those prosaic items that philosophers call material objects: chairs, tables, inkstands and the like. But these objects are to be attended to solely as occurring within experience.

Although this specification may seem too broad to be useful, underneath, we can discern a concentration upon a certain type of inquiry. Our attention is only to those objects that *appear* within experience and we attend only to how they appear. What seems confusing at first is that given objects of experience may not only be many—tables, chairs, inkstands, *ad infinitum*—but any one object of experience may appear in different ways—perceived through the senses, imagined, remembered, hypothesized, etc. Yet this is precisely the first point: the whole of experience may be thus surveyed in its infinite field, as Husserl contended, and the first steps are steps that begin to realize the complexity and immensity of that field.

There is also a second point lurking within the first weighted direction of inquiry. What is sought is what is given; what is sought is what is *immediate* or *present to* the experiencer. Such phenomena as "appearances" are certain, or *apodictic*, as the tribal language puts it. Apodictic here means simply that, that which is present, is present in such a way that it shows itself as certainly present. What is immediate or apodictic, however, is also strictly limited to its present givenness. Thus, while it may or may not be the case that the dark shadowy figure I perceive in the hallway really is a person rather than a hatrack, at the moment of the shadow-presentation, I cannot doubt that the presentation is given as I see it, within the limits of the moment of perception.

For philosophers, this very first step is already fraught with latent secondary questions which will ultimately have to be clarified. For example, isn't there a difference between what is "really" the case and what only "appears" to be the case? Isn't it necessary to decide what is sufficient evidence of identity, and only then decide whether the shadowy figure is either a person or a hatrack? Isn't present immediacy illusory and undependable as a basis of knowledge? However, all of these questions, while relevant and important, must be suspended, at first, if phenomenology is to be entered at all. There are phenomenological answers to each of the questions, justifications as affirmative as traditional philosophies would offer, but each answer takes a longer route to explain why such and such must be the case. Thus, if phenomenology is not to founder at the very first step, it is essential that ordinary belief and taken-for-granted theory be suspended so far as to allow glimpses of what will later be seen more fully. Phenomenology calls on us to pretend that what we have as primary, as first given, are these immediate experiences, and to look carefully at them, perhaps more carefully than ever before.

The first operational rule, then, is to attend to the phenomena of experience as they appear. A parallel rule, which makes attention more rigorous, may be stated in Wittgensteinian form: *Describe, don't explain.* This, too, sounds terribly simple, in fact so simple that until it is applied radically, it seems quite trivial. But this seemingly simple rule hides a great amount of complexity, because here, description is meant in a very specific and rigorous way. To *describe* phenomena phenomenologically, rather than *explain* them, amounts to selecting a domain for inclusion and a domain for exclusion. This is a rule that begins to specify the initial goals for phenomenology.

What is excluded is explanation—but what is explanation? In an initial sense, explanation is any sort of theory, idea, concept or construction that attempts to go *behind* phenomena, to give the reason for a phenomenon, or account for it in terms other than what appears. Again, this seems terribly simple until it is actually tried. Let us look at a set of unexpanded initial examples to show the confusions that may arise from the deceptively simple rule of description.

Imagine a classroom in which the teacher asks the students a series of questions about colors. He asks the class, "Is black a color?" Several hands go up; several answers are forthcoming. The first student says, "Yes, it's the opposite of white." A second student says, "No, black is the absence of all colors," and a third student says, "Black is not a physical color, it is not a color really, it just seems to be a color." What, really, is the case? The answer is long and complex and involves what are known as metaphysical commitments. But now, suppose the teacher points at the chalk board and asks, "What color is that?" In this case the answer will probably be unanimous: "Black."

This example is already quite complex, in that the two questions are quite different in terms of the context they set. In the first question, "Is black a color," the temptation to give a metaphysical answer is intrinsic. What *really* is the case? With the second question, "What color is that" the context is confined to ordinary immediacy; ordinary experience is the best judge of the answer. But the metaphysical answer to the first question offers an explanation rather than a description. The type of explanation offered probably depends upon what the students have learned about color from science classes. Ultimately, experienced colors are roughly effects of certain wave lengths of light (such as those that result from the breaking up of white light by a prism) and thus are in themselves "really" not what we see at all. This answer goes behind an apparent phenomenon and explains it by something that is not itself experienced, i.e., the wave lengths of light. In its initial—and I stress initial—phase, phenomenology eliminates any such explanation from its descriptions in order to establish a field of purely present experience.

In some measure this helps create clearer boundaries about what will be discussed. A similar move in analytic philosophies would be delimiting various categories of discourse. For example, if I were to ask, pointing to the ladybug crawling across my table, "What do you see there," and I were to get an answer, "I see red and black stimuli on my retina," not only would I be confused, but I might also say that the answer was a confusion between an explanation and a reported experience.

Now it might seem that phenomenology, not only limits itself to appearances, but further limits itself to the realm of ordinary experience, since in each of the above cases, the ordinary-experience answer was approximate to a phenomenological answer. But this is deceptive: the explanatory answers in the above illustrations may also be said to be ordinary, in that they rely upon widely taken-for-granted knowledge, but even ordinary-experience-contexted answers remain insufficient for phenomenological rigor. What is important to note at this juncture is that one must carefully delimit the field of experience in such a way that the focus is upon describable experience *as* it shows itself. The difficulty to avoid here is a confusion of immediacy with non-experienced elements presumed or posited in explanations.

The philosophically inclined may be disturbed by this second step. Does this mean that all explanation is to be given up? Does this mean that phenomenology is restricted to ordinary experience? Does it mean that phenomenology is anti-scientific, since much science is precisely explanatory rather than descriptive? Again, there are phenomenologically generated answers to each of these questions. But still, the entry into phenomenology in action must be given priority over dealing with each and every objection. Therefore I shall continue to elaborate initial hermeneutic rules.

The third hermeneutic rule may be stated as *horizontalize or equalize all immediate phenomena.* Negatively put, do not assume an initial hierarchy of "realities." In its original form, this part of the phenomenological reductions called for a "suspension of belief" in all existence predicates or beliefs. For obvious reasons, this was one of the hardest of the phenomenological rules of procedure to accept. It was thought to mean that one had to lay aside one's belief in reality itself, in order to do phenomenology. This is a gross misunderstanding of the function of *epoché,* which in phenomenology calls for abstention from certain kinds of belief. *Epoché* requires that looking precede judgment and that judgment of what is "real" or "most real" be suspended until all the evidence (or at least sufficient evidence) is in.

This rule is a critical element of phenomenology and must not be skipped over. It may perhaps be more easily understood if it is seen in terms of its *functions.* First, it functions as an extension of an inclusionary/exclusionary rule of description. Included are all phenomena of experience. Excluded are metaphysical and reality judgments as such. These are suspended. But the rationale for exclusion remains strictly in keeping with the first two rules which require taking careful note of phenomena without either imposing something upon them or too soon concluding something about them. I have stated this hermeneutic rule more positively by calling for the horizontalization of all phenomena at the onset.

By horizontalization, I mean that initially all phenomena must be thought of as "equally real" *within the limits of their givenness*. This procedure prevents one from deciding too quickly that some things are more real or fundamental than other things. An illustration will show what is involved. I turn to conflicting reality beliefs to show how beliefs tend to reduce or distort the full range of appearances, which is the first essential of phenomenological viewing.

Imagine two seers, a "cartesian" seer and a "druidic" seer. Both are assigned the task of observing a series of tree-appearances under a set of varying conditions and reporting what the tree "really" is like. The cartesian seer returns with a very accurate description of the tree's color, the shape of its leaves, the texture of its bark and its characteristic overall shape. However, upon questioning him, we find that out of the conditions under which the tree appearances occurred, the cartesian seer chose as *normative* only appearances in the bright sun on a clear day. His clear and distinct tree, characterized as essentially an extended, shaped, colored configuration, is a cartesian tree, which appears best in the light of day, all other conditions being dismissed as less than ideal for observation.

The druidic seer returns with a quite different description. His tree emerges from an overwhelming nearness of presence and is eery, bespeaking its druid or spirit within. It waves and beckons, moans and groans, advances and retreats. Upon interrogation, it turns out that his *normative* conditions were misty nights and windy mornings in the half-light of dawn, when the tree appeared as a vague shape emerging from the fog or a writhing form in the wind. His tree is a druidic tree; a quiet sunny day fails to reveal the inner tree-reality.

We now have to reconcile the seers, for neither of their arguments will convince the other of what the tree is "really" like. Phenomenologically we discern that the normative appearance conditions that govern what is taken as seeing are very intricately involved with two sets of reality assumptions about trees and their nature. The cartesian seer believes that reality is clear, distinct, extended, colored and shaped. Appearances disproving this belief are ranked as distorted, befogged, unclear, and are rejected as a deficient mode of seeing. The druidic seer holds that appearances in bright sunshine mask the true animated reality of the tree. Mist, wind and rain reveal inner meaning, while bright, daylight appearances are rejected as misleading.

This simplified example shows that each seer sees what he already believes is "out there"; his seeing confirms him in his metaphysics. Phenomenology holds that reality belief must be suspended in order to allow the full range of appearances to show themselves. This is the function of horizontalization.

The three closely related rules I have discussed—(a) attend to phenomena as and how they show themselves, (b) describe (don't explain) phenomena and (c) horizontalize all phenomena initially— tell us something about how a phenomenological investigation must begin at the first level. But they also leave us searching for some criterion of relevance, for if we remain at this point, we can become lost among things. We can describe anything we like *ad infinitum*. This confusion of complexities has some worth, in that it might rekindle genuine philosophical perplexity, an approximation of Aristotle's wonder. But, in order to pursue that wonder, we need to establish a general sense of procedure before undertaking the first concrete investigation.

These rules specify the field, and in a certain sense, function negatively, in that they eliminate certain methodological choices. With the next set of hermeneutic or interpretative rules, forming a second level of procedures, a more active side of the phenomenological investigation emerges.

At this stage, another choice is made. Husserl calls for phenomenologists to look, not just at particularities, but to delve into *essential features* (essences) of phenomena. I shall also refer to these as *structural* features or *invariants* within phenomena.

This second choice, particularly in Husserlian phenomenology, seems to link phenomenology with many of the older philosophical traditions that are concerned with particularity and universality. Clearly, the tribal term "essence" seems to make that connection. Essence is a term which, in traditional philosophy, sometimes means a general character: that which a number of things have in common. Sometimes it means a universal, in the sense that a certain number of things belong to it, while others do not. And sometimes it means a condition without which a thing would not be what it is. All of these meanings have their place within phenomenology, but other meanings also arise, such as, "inexact essences" which mean that a thing *positively* lacks precise definition, or (better put) its definition *is* its ambiguity. But rather than determining too quickly and narrowly what essence means, one must found its meaning on phenomenological looking itself. The terms "structure" and "invariant features" should neutralize too quick an identification with other traditions. What this hermeneutic device demands is that phenomena be looked at with a particular interest, an interest that seeks out essential or structural features. Thus, the fourth hermeneutic rule is: *Seek out structural or invariant features of the phenomena.* In this, phenomenology retains its similarity with empirical science. It looks for the structures of things that appear in the way in which they appear. Repeated patterns are significant and must be actively probed.

Probing, too, must take on a phenomenological form. The probing activity of investigation is called *variational method.* Husserl's preferred tool was what he called "fantasy" variations. These variations were modeled on familiar logical and mathematical practices. Thus to solve a problem, the phenomenologist must go through all the variations that will lead to an adequate insight or solution. But as later phenomenologists pointed out, investigations of regions of experience show that there are sometimes significant differences between the various dimensions of experience. Perceptual variations often contrast with imaginative or conceptual variations, though the activity of varying what is investigated is retained. The method to be used in this book relies upon perceptual experience for the most part.

In its simplest form, the use of variations requires obtaining as many *sufficient* examples or variations upon examples as might be necessary to discover the structural features being sought. This device is not unknown to other philosophies and sciences. Empirical investigations always seek out a series of examples prior to generalization, and contemporary philosophies are quite fond of citing paradigm examples and counter-examples to illustrate the certainty or doubtfulness of a philosopher's claim. However, free variations employed in a systematic way are a central methodological feature of all phenomenological investigation.

Two initial forewarnings should accompany an introduction to variational method. First, the variations must genuinely belong together. Each step of the procedure must be completed prior to wider extrapolation. Once an insight is gained through the use of variations, extrapolation becomes easier and easier as more recognized structural features are accumulated. Second and more seriously, it must be recognized that it is extremely difficult to judge the point at which variations are sufficient. (Later on, phenomenological "levels" and the problem of closure which they pose for all genuine phenomenological investigation will be encountered.)

One objective of the variational method parallels that desired in the horizontalization of phenomena. Variations "possibilize" phenomena. Variations thus are devices that seek the invariants in variants and also seek to determine the limits of a phenomenon. Ideally, of course, variations should be infinite, but fortunately, this is not necessary since a sufficient number of observations usually yields the essential features.

Return to the example of the tree-observers. In contrast to both the cartesian and druidic seers, the user of variational method gives primary value to the full range of possible tree-appearances. He realizes that it is only through a complete series of possible tree-appearances that essential features may be discerned.

In both the lowest level of hermeneutic rules (which specify the field) and the second level of activity rules (which specify what and how something is to be focused upon), phenomenology resembles an empirical science. It is "empirical" in the sense that it is observational in the first instance; it is "scientific" in that its interest is in the structure of a given phenomenon; and it is "psychological" in that its primary field is that which occurs within experience.

So far, I have been discussing *phenomenological reductions*, those methodological devices that clear the field and specify how it is to be approached. However, a more total possibility may also be attained. If phenomenology is to become *philosophical*, it must make a more total claim to significance in its choices. Such a move, again adopting the language of Husserl, is made by elevating all the previous hermeneutic rules to the level of the *transcendental*. Following the older tradition of Immanuel Kant, what is needed is *a condition for the possibility* of the type of phenomena that show themselves within the phenomenological view. This condition must also be an invariant feature of overall experience, the fundamental structure of experience.

Husserl's claim was that *intentionality* was precisely that structure and precisely that feature of experience overall, which make possible the way in which phenomena can and do appear. Intentionality as transcendental is the condition of the possibility for all experience to be shaped in a certain way. To introduce intentionality at this juncture may be premature. But, by anticipating what for phenomenology is *the* shape of experience, there can be gained a glimpse of overall direction. Intentionality summarizes all that has gone before in this initial framework. Intentionality is the directional shape of experience.

I should like to introduce the terminology concerning intentionality in a preliminary and somewhat unusual way. Rather than describing how intentionality is arrived at in the history of phenomenology, I should like to include its *function* as the ultimate hermeneutic rule by which phenomenology operates. It is the rule that specifies the horizon or boundary of phenomenology within which the totality of things may be dealt with. Intentionality *functions* as a correlational rule, and in his later works, Husserl sometimes spoke of intentionality as *correlation-apriori*. An *apriori* is the ground level that founds all other levels; it may also be considered the limit beyond which phenomenology ceases to be itself. Thus I shall continue to look at the way in which phenomenology functions, now from the point of view of operating according to a *correlational rule.*

This higher-level correlation rule is nothing more than a further explication of what was implicit in the lower-level rules. The correlation-apriori extends fully and universalizes what was latent in the descriptive strategy of the previous procedures. It makes a universal claim, which moves phenomenology from a regional method and claim (descriptive psychology) to a philosophy.

A correlation rule implies a correlation of something with something. Given a field of (possible) experience, the question is first, what is to be correlated with what and second, how the correlation is to be interpreted. In traditional philosophies, a distinction is usually made between object and the subject that knows the object. Husserl transformed this distinction into a correlation of what is experienced with its mode of being experienced. He termed the correlation itself *intentionality.* He held that such a correlation was, in fact, invariant to experience and that this correlation could be thought of as directed. All experience is experience of_____. This is to say, all experiencing implies something that is experienced, but within this general concept of experience, two poles can be differentiated descriptively. In an ordinary sense, then, if I am to examine a time-span of my experience, I can, according to Husserl, distinguish within this experience those items, or *things of experience,* which present themselves to me (at this moment, for example, I see the typewriter, my desk top, the pens, papers and pencils appear on my desk). The *way* in which these things are present to me (for example, the typewriter appears to me as before me, referring itself to the position I occupy in relation to it; its "b" key is sticking because of the humid weather here in the woods, referring me to my feeling of its resistance to touch, etc.). But while these differentiations may be made, they remain strictly relative or *relational* distinctions: *every experiencing has its reference or direction towards what is ex-*

perienced, and, contrarily, *every experienced phenomenon refers to
or reflects a mode of experiencing to which it is present.* This is the
intentional or correlation apriori of experience taken phenomenologically.

Husserl gave the two sides of this correlation names which have
become traditional. For what is experienced, as experienced, he
used the term *noema* or noematic correlate, and for the mode of experiencing which is detected reflexively, he used the term *noesis* or
noetic correlate. (Noema and noesis, as used here, and in distinction
to the highly technical uses later developed by Husserl, refer simply
to the two sides of the correlation rule. They are foci within overall
experience, or correlational poles.)

This internal correlation within experience may seem trivial and
obvious—if I experience at all, I experience something and in some
way. But, in order not to fall outside the boundaries being circumscribed for the phenomenological investigation, note that the correlation applies to and is found in all the various types of observation
we include under the name of human experience. Thus, perceptually, I may see something—the typewriter before me, feel it as resist-
ing me, particularly the letter "b"—in a certain way. At the same
time, I may imaginatively visualize a green bottlefly buzzing before
me. This imaginary noema has its own specific character as imagined, and I detect reflectively, that for it to continue its phenomenological presence before me, I must actively renew it imaginatively.
Even emotionally (though mood is not a "representation" of something), a certain mood is present to me in that it gives a color or
shade to the whole of the immediate context. In each of these situations, a dimension of experience has its directional and referential
focus: it is *intentional.*

However, in this preliminary look at phenomenology, I am em-
phasizing the correlation of noematic and noetic aspects of experience. This correlation may be simplified as the following set of dia-
grams show. If what is experienced as experienced (the noema) is
placed on one side of a correlation, then the mode of its being ex-

perienced (noesis) is always strictly parallel to it. One does not, and cannot, occur without the other. This correlation of noema with noesis may be diagrammed:

noesis ─────▶ noema

Here, noema stands for that which is experienced. The arrow indicates that this experience is directed or referential, and its particular shape in the "how" experienced, is indicated by noesis. Within the phenomenological reduction, then, only that which is so correlated is considered.

Judging from ordinary interpretation of experience, the diagram seems incomplete. It might well be granted that there is always that which is experienced, and, even, that which is the mode of experiencing. However, in an ordinary interpretation, one would also expect to find a *bearer* of experience, a subject, the concrete "I" who does the experiencing. Thus to complete the diagram it seems a third term is needed:

(I)noesis ─────▶ noema
(experiencer) experiencing-experienced

The correlation now seems complete: a relation between myself as the experiencer and something which is present as experienced. At the inception of Husserl's work in phenomenology, something like this was developed. The "I" was for Husserl, the *ego* interpreted as the thinking self. In fact, in the midst of what has been called his egological period, Husserl formulated the correlation as:

Ego–cogito–cogitatum

This defines the correlation as the ego (thinking self) thinking what is thought. However, for my purposes, I have placed the "I" in parenthesis, a modification of the original Husserlian form of the correlation, for reasons that will soon become apparent.

If I begin now to take note of my experience, deliberately trying to find the most straightforward experience possible, I may well make a certain discovery. In most of my straightforward experiences, I am certainly not primarily, or even self-consciously, attentive to what is going on in that experience. Instead, I am busy attending to the matter at hand. Thus, if I am chopping wood for the evening fire in Vermont, I am so involved with splitting the wood, that I do not notice much of what goes on around me, nor do I think self-consciously about how it is that I am splitting the wood. In fact, if I do turn critical and self-conscious, while my ax is raised to swing, I may miss the log entirely.

But, after the fact, I may note in this simple report that I can distinguish and easily move between what appears to be two variations within experience. Straightforward experience, I could and did characterize: it was actional, involved, immersed in the project of the moment, narrowly focused and concentrated. My thinking about that experience, also an experience in the general sense, was a *reflection* or a *thematizing* of the straightforward experience. These two modes of experience are familiar and easily alternate in the ongoing affairs of the day.

This apparently simple distinction between straightforward experience and reflective experience can, however, be misleading. In the straightforward experience, I am involved with things; the straightforward experience is "real," while in the reflective experience, I have already stepped outside "real" experience and begun to think *about* experience—perhaps implying that I am in some sense outside or above experience. Phenomenological reporting is done reflectively. Thinking *about* experience presupposes both some form of experience as its subject matter and some kind of distance from that subject matter in order to thematize it. Thus, in some phenomenology, the reflective move is characterized as a move outside or above or distanced from straightforward experience.

This was the way in which Husserl characterized an early phenomenological version of what I shall call the *reflexive move*.[4] Husserl maintained that phenomenological reporting was done in terms of a modification of reflective thinking, a thinking *about* experience which presupposes some other form of experience as its noema, and some kind of distance in order to thematize that experience. Thus, Husserl frequently characterized the reflective stance as outside or above ordinary or straightforward experience. Here the "I" transcends straightforward experience and was called a "transcendental ego." Were I to make a diagram of this interpretation following our first correlation, it would appear thus:

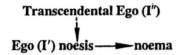

We have here an enigma. On the one hand, the whole correlation is the noema for the transcendental ego (I"). Conversely, the transcendental ego (I") is interpreted as above and outside the correlation. But if the correlation is itself the ultimate structural feature of human experience, then this transcendental move is questionable. On the other hand, there remains a sense in which the transformation of reflection upon experience still retains the correlation structure, in that the transcendental ego is actually only a modification of the ordinary ego (I') and, as transcendental ego, must be correlated with the new noema. This feature might be diagrammed as:

Transcendental Ego (I″) noesis ——►noema

                                (Ego-noesis-noema theme)

But this reduces the "outside" and "above" of the transcendental ego to the simple (I) noesis-noema correlation, and makes the transcendental interpretation unnecessary.

This excursus merely records part of the history of phenomenology. Almost all Husserl's followers rejected the transcendental interpretation he gave the ego and turned in what has become known as an existential direction.

Transcendental phenomenology gave way to *existential phenomenology*. I, too, shall ultimately follow this direction, but in such a way, I hope, as to be able to justify why this modification of Husserl is called for. What can now be noted is that a certain general shape for overall experience has emerged. Intentionality as the *direction* of experience within its correlation has a limit and a shape.

This field and shape of intentionality might be conceived in a diagram as an ellipse with two foci:

The field of overall experience is indicated by the ellipse. Since every possible experience falls within the ellipse, strictly speaking nothing lies outside it. Within the ellipse (overall experience) there are two related foci (what is experienced and that to which what is experienced refers). The lines of relation indicate the possible modes of experience. Intentionality is the name for the direction and internal shape of experience. Reflection is the means of bringing forth the specifics of that direction and shape.

We need a somewhat finer discrimination of what happens in reflection. I return to straightforward experience. If I consider the most intense experience and if I make a careful description, I note that any usual sense of "I" is not at all thematized—although I cannot say that I am *unaware* of myself in any total sense. In the woodchopping, my primary energy and concentration is focused *almost* totally in the project itself. In such a situation, I say that I am not *self-conscious*, but this is not to say that I am unaware of being-in-a-situation. I might even go on to describe this situation as one in which "I" should be put roughly as "I-am-in-the-ax-directed-towards-the-wood," or, paraphrasing Merleau-Ponty, "I am outside myself in the world of my project."

To say that self-consciousness is reduced to a minimum, that the "I" of such experiences is not thematized or explicit, is not at all to say that such experiences are lacking in awareness or are opaque.

47

Quite to the contrary, in ordinary or mundane life, such experiences can be a vivid example of the most valued type of experience. In reporting in the ordinary mode, I might well recall such occasions as those when "I was most alive. . . ." The "I," in such situations, is the "I" that is most thoroughly involved and enters into the project at hand in such a way that its self-consciousness is reduced to a minimum. Yet, I recognize that the intense involvement experienced must be identified with the "I" which I do thematize in my ordinary—and my phenomenological—reflections. However, because the thematization of this "I" comes afterward, it cannot be made the first element or the most obvious element in the descriptive analysis made in reflection.

From this it can be seen why the "I" in the correlational scheme at the straightforward level was placed within parenthesis. The "I," particularly in its thematized form, comes late in the analysis rather than being given as a first. This is to say, the "I" has a certain genesis or recognizable origin in the movements of experience. But let us now retrace the movement from straightforward experience to a reflection upon that experience.

In my description of chopping wood as a straightforward experience, the most dramatic aspect was the involvement with a range of things concentrated into what appeared, reflectively, as a pattern of relationships. While chopping wood, my perceptual attention is concentrated upon the piece of wood to be cut. The piece of wood absorbs my attention and stands out from the entire environment around me. This is not to say that the piece of wood is all that remains within my awareness, but only that it forms the focal core. I may secondarily be aware of the ax and the aim directed through it—but, if I am a skilled wood chopper, this will be barely noticeable. (Conversely, the beginner, who is more aware of the ax and is concerned about hitting the wood just right, allows an "ax-awareness" to intrude, so that he may miss the wood entirely or slice at it rather than cut it.) What stands out as "first" and takes preeminence in such performances, is the *terminal* element of the correlation, the noematic terminus. Thus, as shown in the diagram below, the *noema* in the normative, straightforward experience is that which first appears or stands out within the entire field of possible experience. This noematic focal presence in straightforward experience provides a direction for the inquiry. Its initial primacy opens the way for an order to phenomenological description. I note this initial primacy as:

$$\text{(I)noesis} \longrightarrow \text{noema}$$
$$1$$

I can associate a secondary rule with this precedence: begin observation and description with that which "first" appears in straightforward experience; this is the noematic correlate. It is thus "to the things" that phenomenology turns.

But this initial precedence does not abolish the correlation. Whatever is experienced in a straightforward mode may be reflexively related to the mode of experiencing, which is also open to reflective access. In fact, what stands out within straightforward experience is often quite transparently correlated with what I do, with my turning of attention to this or that thing. Some simple variations show this.

I may be concentrating intensely upon something that does not make any obvious demand upon me. Listening to music, I can make the strains of the oboe stand out from the quartet, even though its voice is recessive when compared with that of the French horn. Or I may be attending to something, when suddenly something else forces my attention elsewhere—while I am listening to the oboe against the stronger strains of the horn, suddenly some other listener in the audience stands up and shouts "Boo," and my attention is instantaneously altered to correlate with this surprising phenomenal demand.

In these instances I have emphasized my attention and its changes and variations. In doing this, I have begun to move toward the second or noetic pole of the correlation. Each appearance appears in a certain way, always relationally to my degree and type of attention. This is part of the noetic correlation. This movement from noema towards noesis provides a second step in the order of the analysis.

From any noema I can move towards a noesis, and thus the initial primacy of things can lead to its correlated noetic component:

$$(I)\text{noesis} \longrightarrow \text{noema}$$
$$2———— 1$$

The analysis begins with *what* appears (noema) and then moves *reflexively* towards its *how* of appearing.

What appears (the strains of the oboe appearing against the background of the quartet) does so in a certain configuration. Essential to how it appears is this standing out as a core phenomenon against the background phenomenon of the quartet. I listen for the oboe, in spite of the horn; I focus in on the oboe. This is my noetic activity, which allows or actively constitutes the condition for the oboe's standing out. But I note this form of the activity only with respect to what is attended to. Its possibilities are revealed by way of the oboe-quartet configuration. Thus the shape of the noetic possibility is arrived at by way of the noematic possibility. Noesis appears *reflexively*.

There is but one more step to the process. It concerns the "I". How is the "I" "constituted," as Husserlian language would have it? It is constituted as the noetic terminus, the structured bearer of experience. To diagram the "I" within the correlation is now possible:

$$(I)\text{noesis} \longrightarrow \text{noema}$$
$$3 — 2———— 1$$

Here, then, is the order for analysis. Analysis moves from that which is experienced towards its reflexive reference in the how of experience, and terminates in the constitution of the "I" as the correlated counterpart of the noema. The "I" is a late arrival in the phenomenological analysis. In this respect, phenomenological analysis is the inverse of introspective analysis. The "I" is arrived at not directly, but by way of reflexivity. An introspective ego or "I" claims direct, immediate and full-blown self-awareness as an initial and given certain. In phenomenology, the "I" appears by means of and through reflection upon the phenomena that in toto are the world. Put in ordinary terms, the phenomenological "I" takes on its significance through its encounter with things, persons, and every type of otherness it may meet.

This may be seen partially in terms of the correlational scheme itself, now that the order of analysis has been settled. The rationale of the order of analysis comes from the analysis of experiences I have been making. A return to the difference between straightforward and reflective experience may show how the order may be interpreted. Reflective reporting, it was noted, presupposed and in some instances was dependent upon, straightforward experience. To reflect is to reflect about something, which is to say, in phenomenological language, that reflection is intentional. Reflection, too, has a directive or "outward" aim towards certain noema: those that are a previous (or even simultaneous) experience. The modification occurring in this type of reflection is not a modification of the correlation; it is a modification of the noema. The Husserlian positing of a "transcendental ego" is unnecessary, at least with respect to one of its undesirable implications.

Were there to be an "I" somehow above and outside the correlation, rather than constituted reflexively within the correlation, phenomenology would revert to a kind of metaphysical stance it wishes to avoid. If intentionality is not something merely subjective, but is the very means of access to the world, then any observer above or outside the correlation must be a philosopher's god, or some form of ideal observer. But this is precisely what the phenomenological reductions must exclude. Furthermore, if the philosopher is the person who is involved in the correlation itself, then access to the ideal observation can be had only within the correlation, intentionally.

Here I am anticipating the *existential* transformation of phenomenology. Just as Kierkegaard complained that Hegel had proceeded to construct a grand System and then sat down outside it, forgetting that the philosopher was a human being, so the existential transformation of phenomenology maintains that any "ego" must be concrete. But more is involved than that. The existential phenomenological position maintains that the essential insight of phenomenology is lost unless this correlation is strictly maintained.

In the existential version of the reflexive turn, the "I" remains constantly involved with its projects, except that in a reflection upon experience, the involvement is with a previous or different element within overall experience. In the second diagram on page 46, however, the transcendental position of I″ has disappeared, and the diagram simply preserves the initial correlation apriori of intentionality. This is to say that reflective experience retains certain characteristics of every straightforward experience. It has its own mode of involvement, in which the "I" of reflective experience is as involved (and as hidden) as the only implicit "I" of straightforward experience. But it remains the case that something has changed, and this is what is remarkable about reflective experience and gives it at least an initial philosophical advantage. Reflective experience can and does thematize and reflect upon other experience, giving a possibility of self-distancing within overall experience. But the way in which self-distancing occurs must not do violence to the original intentional correlation.

The distancing within experience that is self-distancing is an *internal* difference within the correlation. And the reflexive turn derives its shape from the "mirror" of the world as the totality of noematic possibilities. This existential interpretation of intentionality permits a more rigorous maintenance of the insight of the correlation apriori, and founds the stance from which phenomenological inquiry takes its view.

With this framework in mind, one of the puzzles over the initial choice made within phenomenological theory can be put in perspective. From the point of view of ordinary interpretation, itself already containing the sediment of a long tradition of metaphysical belief, a distinction between "reality" and "appearance" is needed to account for occurrences such as mistakes. For example, at the beginning of this chapter, I referred to a perception of a shadowy presence that could have been either a hatrack or a person. How does one decide which is real and which only apparent? The answer may now be seen to require a more probing inquiry, which includes a reformulation of the question itself.

By setting aside the ordinary interpretation and substituting for it an interpretation within the framework of a correlation theory, we see that what counts as evidence, and what counts in how that evidence is obtained, is of utmost importance. The most naive form of objectivist answer will assume a need for a philosopher's god or ideal observer, declaring that the truth of the situation can be seen from "above," from the point of view of an ideal observer who will know what the shadowy shape "really" is. But this will not do on two grounds. First, I, the concrete observer, am not the god; and second, were such a god needed, I would still have to get access to him from the limits of my actual situation. Thus I would find myself wondering whether he were genuinely reporting a reality or whether he were the evil genius of Modern Philosophy as per Descartes.

In contrast, if the question is reformulated from a phenomenological position, all I can assume is the stance of my actual position vis-à-vis the world. The development of a dependable and viable distinction between "reality" and "appearance" would then have to come out of a further analysis of the experiential context itself. Could it be that experience, insofar as "truth" is attainable, must correct itself? Do not I, as an actual observer, ultimately decide whether the shadowy figure is a hatrack or a man only by further and more adequate observation? Must not the correction of perceptual mistakes ultimately come from perception, just as the correction of logical mistakes comes from further logical inquiry? At least if this is the case, all that it is necessary to presuppose is the limited situation of being human. What is problematic is the clarification of that situation and its genuine possibilities, and this is the direction which a reformulation of questions addressed to preliminary reservations takes.

Up to this point, a very general and necessarily abstract outline has been offered concerning the question of how phenomenology is to approach the first questions of experience. Seen from this point of view, phenomenology is an examination of experience that deals with and is limited by whatever falls within the correlation of experienced-experiencing. It proceeds in a prescribed order, starting from what appears as it appears, and questions retrogressively from the what of appearance to the how of experience and ultimately back to the who of experience. The hermeneutic rules establish a strictly descriptive interpretation of experience, which eschews explanation and all hypothetical constructions relying upon, presupposing or seeking to establish accounts of experience that go behind or above experience. Although the critical mind may anticipate problems at each juncture, the next task is to begin the initial observations which call for *doing* phenomenology.

Notes

1. Edmund Husserl, *Cartesian Meditations*, pp. 12–13.

2. Martin Heidegger, *Being and Time*, p. 51.

3. Martin Heidegger, *Being and Time*, p. 50.

4. Edmund Husserl, *The Crisis of European Sciences and Transcendental Phenomenology*, translated by David Carr (Evanston: Northwestern University Press, 1970), p. 150.

Chapter Three

The Visual Field:
First Phenomenological Excursus

Although not all terms have been introduced, it is now possible to begin an excursus into experience. In this chapter, I shall introduce terms pertaining to structures by way of a visual model. However, despite much philosophical and psychological tradition, dealing with vision in isolation is phenomenologically suspect. Thus, a turn to a visual model must itself be attained phenomenologically.

When I first turn to experience, the problem is one of orientation—to what experience? There seems to be so much of it. How do I orient myself amidst what William James called a "blooming, buzzing confusion"? Mindful that the very questions I put to experience determine a direction, I must take account of its very breadth and complexity.

To meet this requirement, I will make a *catalogue* of momentary experience, trying to note as much as possible of what occurs within a short span of experience.

I take this morning as my point of departure and reflect upon my awakening. What first strikes my attention is the sound of rain falling on the roof of my summer cabin. But rain does not fall without significance, and I am immediately aware of its meaning. Since it is raining, pouring the foundations for the larger house will again be delayed. I become aware of my own feelings of frustration. But these two different phenomena do not exhaust the situation. In contrast to the rain and my frustration, I am aware that my wife lies beside me, still asleep, warm and comforting. And in the midst of all this are numerous fleeting events as well. A yellowthroated warbler has just appeared at the window; there are vague stirrings of hunger within my body; there are the sounds of the children making a fire in the stove, etc. Thus my first impression of a span of experience is one of vast complexity and multiplicity. It is a Joycean stream of consciousness which would take pages to elaborate fully.

I make a more careful examination of this initial reflection. I note that although a short experience span is immensely complex, not everything stands out equally, or is equally demanding. I note that my awareness tends to flit from one concern to another, sometimes with great rapidity, sometimes slowly. This flow of events has at least a minimal structure or pattern. Its multiplicities range from that which stands out to that which is on the fringe of my consciousness.

Taking this as a clue, I now turn to a typical philosophical device. I return to experience seeking to simplify it, to reduce it to a manageable dimension. Rather than continue with the vastness of global experience, which is clearly primary, I choose to concentrate solely upon what I see, upon visual phenomena. After all, nothing is simpler than this because I am familiar with the tradition of the five separable senses. But immediately, if I remain strictly phenomenological and attend carefully to the full phenomena, I find something difficult in what I thought simple. I find that I cannot attend solely to vision. No matter how hard I try, the world does not appear to me in a single visual dimension. My global awareness refuses to disappear, and even as I am casting my gaze about me, there remains on the fringes of my awareness the felt weightiness of my body on the bed, the smell of smoke now coming from the fire, and the growing concern with breakfast. I do not and cannot simply rid myself of these presences.

Yet, in spite of this, I am able to *concentrate* my attention upon the visual dimension. The other phenomena do not disappear, their recalcitrant presence remains, but they recede to the fringe of awareness. Simplification is approached but not attained. But I discover a pattern. Just as I was able to concentrate upon the oboe within the quartet, upon the flitting pattern of concerns upon awakening, so I can concentrate upon a visual dimension while mindful that this concentration is not exclusive and does not abolish the full range of global presence. Clearly it is possible to order things in a scale so that some phenomena stand out and others recede.

Again I return to my experiential exercise, now with phenomenology in mind, and I discover that I have not followed the strict order of description. My reflections have been ordinary in that I have mixed noematic and noetic correlates and have taken the "I" for granted. I have not begun the requisite precise analysis. I now begin to break up the experiential elements into their components, taking note first of noematic features within the visual dimension. Whatever "I" language remains should be taken only as the narrative background to the description.

I look upward towards the ceiling. There is a spider on a small web in the corner of the rafter. This spider and its web stand out as a phenomenon. Its appearance is clear and distinct—but not without a context. Its standing out is clearly relative or relational to that against which it stands out, in this case the rafter and the ceiling boards. This relation, already well known to Gestalt psychology (which was a stepchild of early phenomenology), is a figure-ground relation. I seek variations upon this situation. The same pattern is revealed in a series of items I look at: the alarm clock related to its background of nightstand and wall, the hummingbird now at the window against its background of spruce and fir trees. Wherever I turn, that which stands out visually does so against a background and within a context. I begin to sense an invariance to this visual situation.

Pursuing this invariance, I recall a previous example from the classroom. I went to the blackboard and drew the following figure in chalk:

I asked the class what they saw. The first and ordinary response was, of course, "an 'x'." The answer was, in the ordinary context, quite correct. But then I asked, "Is that *all* you see?" Obviously, the answer had to be "no." Each student saw more than an "x"; he saw an "x" on-a-blackboard, which in turn was on-the-wall, which in turn was surrounded-by-the-floor-and-ceiling, which in turn gave way to certain desks and other students, depending on which came within the observer's field of vision.

Here a movement is being made, in spite of seeming triviality, towards phenomenological description. Yet what more obvious observation can there be than that "x's", spiders and alarm clocks appear *only* against a background and *only* in relation to that background? Still, this observation is not necessarily obvious *until it is pointed out*. In fact, were we to do constant variations upon this first simple observation and eventually (adequately) conclude that whatever item appears, *appears only as situated within and against a background*, we should already be upon the verge of making one phenomenological philosophical point. Negatively, and in restricted form, it might be put: *There are no things-by-themselves in the realm of visual presence*, positively: *all items that appear do so in relation to a background and in strict relation with that background.*

This observation is the first intimation of a noematic structural *invariant*. Things as individual items show themselves as related to and situated within a *field*. A thing is relationally determined in this way, and the very notion of a thing-by-itself is at least perceptually an abstraction which belies the full perceptual phenomenon.

But there is something else to notice concerning the appearance of the thing situated within its field: certain things stand out, are focally present, have greater perceptual clarity within central vision. These things are a *core* within the total visual phenomenon. Here I continue to speak about what shows itself, without regard to how this showing comes about. Noematically, what is seen is seen as standing out, as situated at the center of vision, as most explicit.

Moreover, the terms field and core are related. The thing that stands out as the core item within vision does so against the background (field) which is its context. Thus *core* and *field* are relational or paired terms concerning what I see.

Now I return to what is seen to discern other features of the visual panorama and attempt a further series of variations. This time, I will try to detect other significant shapes in the things that appear.

I look straight ahead at my fingers. Keeping my gaze fixed straight ahead, I move my finger sideways. I note that when it was in front of me its appearance was clear and distinct and that as it moves to the side, the distinctness gradually lessens, although I can still detect it and note that it can still be distinguished from its background. However, at some point, the visual appearance of the finger disappears, not at any sharp or all-at-once point, but by an almost undetected withdrawal. I move my finger in several directions and discover that the same thing happens whether I move it to the right, to the left, above my head or at my feet.

What is being evidenced here is the well-known phenomenon of the shape of the *visual field*. This field has a shape with a border or *horizon*. (Note that in phenomenology "horizon" means limit, and so cannot be said to expand or be extended, as in ordinary English.) The shape is roundish. Experiments such as this indicate that there are boundaries to the visual panorama. Any visual phenomenon, as present, occurs only inside or within the field which is situated before and only partly around my bodily position. Furthermore, although I do not ordinarily take note of this, the phenomena appearing at the edges of the field are usually vague and barely noticeable (with known exceptions, such as flashing lights or fast motions) and fade off into the indistinct horizon of the field. Finally, I note that the shape of the field never varies, whatever my bodily position in the world. It is always before me and retains the same configuration for me, regardless of which way I turn.

Now it is possible to come to another conclusion concerning differences within the visual field. The field is bounded by, and situated within a horizon, which has a more or less recognizable shape in spite of its indistinct outline. Thus, in addition to core and field, we have a third term: the paired field located within a horizon or *fringe*. This series of relationship is simplified in the following diagram, representing the visual panorama before me within which all visual phenomena appear:

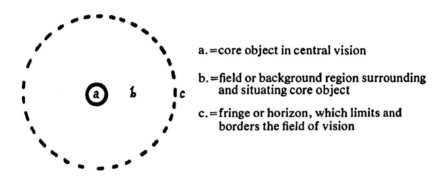

a. = core object in central vision

b. = field or background region surrounding and situating core object

c. = fringe or horizon, which limits and borders the field of vision

I take note of internal relations within the visual field and discern that graded differences occur in ordinary seeing. First, I note as before, that what appears most clearly is at the core of the field and is centrally located, and that those phenomena located nearer the fringe are barely noticed, vague, or difficult to discriminate. To make the latter appear clearly, I must turn my head or cast my eyes upon them, allowing them to be situated within the central core of the visual panorama. I note that in ordinary situations it is possible to overlook or almost forget fringe phenomena altogether. Unless asked about them, I might well be unaware of them. This possibility of ignoring or forgetting fringe phenomena is important, and is a source of much error and distortion in dealing with all phenomena.

In the process initiated here, I have begun to move from first concerns with the appearance of items within the visual field, towards more general structures of the field of appearance itself. In phenomenological terms, this is the movement towards *eidetic* phenomenology or towards the concern with structures or invariants. The structures I have noted belong to the ordinary visual field; descriptively, they make sense of the flow of experience. Structures shape the possibilities of what is seen. In the visual example, the condition of the possibility for visual appearances is the shape and structure of this visual field.

What has been described above are structures within which visual appearances occur. If I generalize—which is possible only after more variations and an intensive search for counter-examples—and if the above structures hold—I can then say that these are structures of *what* is seen *as* it is seen. But precisely at this point, it is equally possible to pass over to a noetic analysis. For every point of the noematic appearance-structure of the visual panorama, a parallel set of descriptions may be made concerning the *act* of seeing. Thus, corresponding to the phenomenon which stands out in the center of the visual field, there is the act of *focusing* which I do. Moreover, this focusing can be done only within certain limits, beyond which is a fringe where focusing is no longer possible.

In most situations the thing I am actively focusing upon stands out in the core of the visual field. But there are other situations in which I respond to something in the rest of the field. If there is a bright flash off to the side, I may turn my head immediately to look for what has occurred. But in any case, whether I look for a thing actively or whether my looking follows some occurrence out there, the relation of core-focus retains a distinctive structural shape.

It turns out, then, that what is arrived at through this descriptive analysis is something more than might have been initially expected. The structure of the visual field, now considered noetically, is the structure of my visual opening to the world, that which determines and limits what and how I see. But take careful account of how this knowledge has been reached. It has not been reached directly or by accepting common belief or direct introspection. Noetically, the conclusion has been reached *reflexively*. It has been by, through, and in terms of the noematic appearances and their structures that this *existential* structure of my opening to the world has been reached.

Now, I have deliberately replaced *reflection* with *reflexivity* to emphasize the way in which ultimate self-knowledge is attained within the phenomenological procedure. I know myself only in correlation with and through the world to which I am intentionally related. This is to say, in phenomenological terms, I and world are correlated, that without world there is no I and without I there is no world (humanly conceived).

The visual world I have lightly sketched is present *for* me in a certain way and, conversely, my access to it is limited in terms of my opening to that "world." The specific shape of the correlation is the condition for my seeing things in the way they are seen. And this shape or structural feature was arrived at through a descriptive analysis of what appeared and how it appeared.

At this point some of the general features of the visual field have been noted, including two sets of noematic relations: the relation of core to field (of centered thing to its background or context) and a relation of the entire field to its fringe (horizon). If these observations are now put in their Husserlian context, it may be said that any thing seen, is seen against its background (external horizon), which etches out its distinctiveness as a figure.

With these larger features in mind, it is now possible to take a narrower look at things. I return to my examination of visual phenomena, this time casting my gaze upon a book lying upon the desk. The book appears as colored (blue), textured (cloth-like), having a certain thickness (about an inch). On its cover are a title and a name. I turn it over. Some of the previously noted characteristics remain, but now the title and name have disappeared from view, and the books presents a different *profile.*

If I pay close attention to this appearance, however, I also note that in the reversal of profiles there remains a *sense* in which the book retains its appearance as *having a backside.* In other words, in the thick, weightiness of the phenomenon-book, I continue to detect something of that which is visually absent from me. Variations can establish this sense. Note what would happen were there not this sense of absence-within-presence. First, I would be most surprised and shocked if I picked up the book and found it had no other side, that it disappeared when I turned it over. I would be surprised, but less so, if it turned out that what I thought to be the weightiness of the book was a clever disguise and that it was only a picture of a book (as in *trompe d'oeil* paintings). In short, the absence-within-presence which is part of the sense of the phenomenon-book is a specific kind of absence. A particular possibility belongs to the phenomenon. Even though *manifestly* presented as a profile *fulfilled* by one's looking, the book also presents a *latent* sense along with what is manifest. It has, in Husserl's language, an *inner* horizon. A complete phenomenon, then, has both a manifest profile and a latent sense. It should be noted that such an analysis is markedly different from any analysis dealing solely with the manifest presence of a phenomenon. The latter, from a phenomenological point of view, is incomplete. I do not see the world without "thickness" nor do I see it as a mere facade. What appears does so as a play of presence and a specific absence-within-presence.

I am introducing here a partial phenomenological account of perception. What is important to note in this account is the co-presence within experience of both a profile and the latently meant absence which, together, constitute the Presence of a thing. To forget or ignore the latent or meant aspect of the Presence of the thing reduces the appearance of the world to a facade, lacking weightiness and opacity. Phenomenologists also claim that what makes any object "transcendent," having genuine otherness, is locatable in this play of presence and absence-in-presence in our perceptions of things. But note that transcendence is constituted *within* experience, experience carefully analyzed.

This characterization of a thing parallels, in a limited and specific way, the previous analysis of the visual field. If I return to the visual field, now fully constituted, I am quite aware in the ordinary sense that my opening to the visual world does not exhaust that world, but is in fact a limited opening. The seeable exceeds what I may see at any given moment or in any given gaze, and this meaning is co-present with my fulfilled seeing. Yet at the same time, whatever I do see (manifest seeing) occurs and only occurs within the limits of my opening to the world. Without the co-present significance of the genuine transcendence of the world in its presence and its absence-in-presence, the world would be a facade for me.

Thus both the transcendence of the thing and the transcendence of the world is to be found in the sense of presence including the specific absence-in-presence that is the inner horizon of the thing on one side and the horizon of the world at the limit. The thing as a "whole" always exceeds my manifest vision, just as the world exceeds my perspective upon the world, and I sense this within and not outside experience.

I have been explaining primarily the noematic meaning of thing and world. However, a noetic correlation is also possible. The sense of transcendence tells me the limits of my opening to the world. I note that my vision is constantly, invariantly, *perspectival*. The constancy of the ratio of manifest profile to latent, but specific, sense reveals reflexively the concreteness of the *position* I occupy. What appears to me, always does so from a certain zero-ground—which I am visually. This seems an obvious discovery: I knew all along that I had a body and eyes and that I was in a certain position vis-à-vis the objects I see. But this is not my point. My point is *how* this knowledge was obtained in the present context. It was obtained reflexively, by way of the things seen, rather than directly. I discover with respect to my position that my perspectival limit, my "point of view," now becomes literally significant because of how the object appears. This retracing of a genesis of self-knowledge, of noesis through noema, is the first step in determining what Husserl called the *constitution of meaning*.

A final (though somewhat ludicrous) example points out this movement from world to I. Imagine that I attained full adulthood without knowing that I had eyes and so did not know what they were like. This notion is absurd, of course, but the absurdity stimulates thought. How *did* I discover what my eyes were like? I might have seen other people with eyes, and as I gradually discovered how like them I was, I may have concluded that I, too, had eyes. Or, I might have made the discovery through the marvel of a mirror. But what if I had no mirror; what if there were no other people with eyes? Hypothetically, I might still discover something about the structure of my eyes by purely reflexive means. From the knowledge I have attained of the shape of the visual field in terms of its noetic correlation, I might at least come to know that my visual opening to the world is roundish. So whatever my eyes might be precisely, since the boundary of my field of vision is roundish, this must be the shape of the opening through which I see. This knowledge, still incomplete, would be sheerly reflexive.

Our first excursus into phenomenological examinations has been modeled around familiar human experience. The visual field, my knowledge of my own body, the gradations and focuses of that experience, all are in some way already known. In terms of phenomenology as such, all I have introduced are certain new terms describing the structures of these experiences more precisely and illustrating the reflexive move in the constitution of self-knowledge.

What has been attained can be illustrated. Here I combine the general programmatic features of the first three chapters with the explication of the visual model of the world in this chapter:

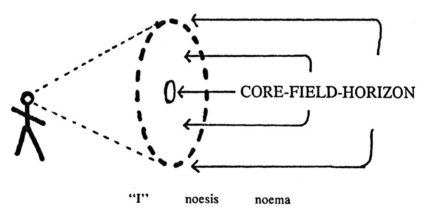

In this objectification, the illustration of the correlational features of I-noesis-noema is visual. The visual field, that totality within which what is seen occurs, is the noematic field. This field is structured in terms of core-field-horizon features. Reflexively, this points back to the particular shape of the visual opening to the world, the noetic structure. Its terminus, reflexively, is the seeing "I," which is already noted to be embodied as a concrete perspective upon the world.

Although what has been developed in this chapter primarily relates to a visual model, it would be apparent that the invariants described here apply to experience in its other dimensions as well. The figure/ground relationship, for example, was noted in auditory experience as the oboe standing out from the quartet. Moreover, there are shape constants to all sensory experience, although this phenomenon has only recently been discussed in the history of thought.

If the familiarity of the visual model makes initial gains simple, this very familiarity has its own kind of resistance, complicating an adequate analysis. Up to now, I have noted what is easily seen, but now is the time to delve more deeply into that which is not so easily seen, but which lies within the richness of the visual phenomenon.

Chapter Four

Illusions and Multi-Stable Phenomena: A Phenomenological Deconstruction

In introducing the programmatic and general features of phenomenological inquiry, I have employed typical philosophers' devices. I have analyzed a totality into components and introduced a simplification. The simplification was a visual model of what is global and complex. I am quite aware that the gains in clarity may be offset by losses in richness. What is pushed to the background or, worse, forgotten, may complicate the investigation in the future. In spite of that, I shall take yet another step towards simplification by making the first area for analysis the so-called visual illusions and multi-stable visual phenomena.

These illusions and multi-stable phenomena are exceedingly familiar, and so deceptively clear. They are the sort of line drawings that appear in both philosophy and psychology textbooks, and even on placemats in restaurants. Some are two-dimensional drawings that appear to be three-dimensional, such as the Necker cube. In others, straight lines appear to be curved. All the line drawings used will be seen to have some kind of visual effect. It will be the task of a concrete phenomenological analysis to deal descriptively with these effects, illustrating in the process how phenomenological analysis goes beyond what is usually taken for granted.

I point out three things about this group of phenomena: (1) These drawings, all familiar in other texts, are simple line drawings and so, abstract. In comparison to fully etched representational line drawings by DaVinci or Michelangelo, they are bare line drawings. This clearly is part of their secret—they are from the outset suggestive in their abstractness. (2) This abstractness is a simplification of ordinary phenomena. Although these phenomena, like every visual phenomenon, display all the qualities of a plenum, they do so in a greatly simplified sense. For example, all visual phenomena show extended phenomenal color. But the multi-shaded phenomenon-tree with its greens, browns, blues and other hues, is a complex color plenum compared to a simple white background with black-line drawings. As Eastern sages have long known, the very blankness allows for effects not easily noted in more filled-in configurations. (3) Abstractness and simplicity are conditions for a certain ease in seeing effects, both in their familiar setting and in the more novel phenomenological setting that emerges from deconstruction. Familiarity and strangeness are here bound closely together. They give rise to perceptual games, which are simple, but not without import for the richer and more complex phenomena that can ultimately be analyzed.

I shall introduce one more simplification. In order to display a step-by-step process, often hard to detect in following actual inquiries, I shall introduce an imaginative context and assume subnormal initial perceptions. This device shows the constructive side of the deconstructions, even though normal perceivers begin at a higher level than my imaginary beginners. We are not considering what we already know; we are considering how what we know is phenomenologically constituted.

These simplifications allow the overall experimental movement of phenomenology to be seen as a movement of discovery. This movement begins with what is apparently given, but in the process of variational investigation, the initial given is progressively deconstructed and then reconstructed according to insights derived from the procedure itself. *Epoché* (the suspension of belief in accepted reality-claims) is assumed, and its function as the opening to discovery is shown. Deconstruction occurs by means of variational method, which possibilizes all phenomena in seeking their structures. In this context, *epoché* includes suspension of belief in any causes of the visual effects and positively focuses upon what is and may be seen. Equally, *epoché* excludes abstract generalizations that may apply to the drawings, but fail to account for the specific effects seen (for instance, the generalization that each example is a two-dimensional line drawing, which is true but trivial). Instead invariants are sought that appear through the variations themselves. With this in mind, the investigation proper may begin.

In what follows I shall name each example according to one of its appearances for ease of reference in subsequent discussion. I shall employ guide pictures, smaller versions of the figures with distinctive features marked on them, in order to avoid elaborate descriptions and make the discussion easier to follow. Neither of these devices is necessary in lectures and teaching, since I can point out what is being discussed. But in the written form, if the reader is to follow the order and be clear about what occurs in each instance, different devices are required. However, the main points should be *seen* in the central, simple line drawings alone. It is important to check your own experience at each step. Of course there are some who will see what is being noted quickly, others less so.

Example One: "The Hallway"

Suppose that there is a group of observers in a room and they are presented with the following drawing:

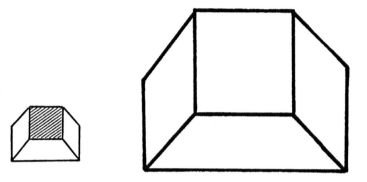

The interrogator who presents the drawing asks, "What do you see?" The response is divided. One group says that what is seen is a *hallway* (in their interpretation of the guide picture, the shaded area appears to be in the rear of the configuration as perceived three-dimensionally); the other group says that what is seen is a cut-off *pyramid* (in their interpretation of the guide picture, the shaded area appears to be forward, with the sides sloping away from it. In this case, the observer's head position approximates a helicopter-pilot overhead). Ordinarily, the hallway-group would see the pyramid appearance in a matter of moments, and vice-versa. But for purposes of analysis, suppose the two groups are kept apart and are stubborn in their belief about the appearance they have seen.

Within the framework of the beginning analysis, what each has seen (noema) may be paired with the, at first, literal-minded way in which the initial appearance is taken, with the following result:

> Group H (hallway group) asserts: The figure *is* a hall-
> way appearance.

> Group P (pyramid group) asserts: The figure *is* a pyra-
> mid appearance.

Although differing about what "really" appears, each of these groups may be characterized as a variation upon a literal-minded impression of an initial appearance. Strictly speaking, the characterization of the way the initial appearance is taken (literal-mindedly) is a characterization of a total attitude. In this context, the specific noesis (a seeing as) occurs. At this point, both groups are at the same level:

Level I.	Noetic Context	Noema
Group H.	literal-mindedness	hallway appearance
Group P.	literal-mindedness	pyramid appearance

Both groups insist doggedly upon the validity of their reality claim with respect to appearance, but, equally, each sees something different in the configuration. Note carefully, however, that each group actually experiences the noema as claimed; they can fulfill or verify this assertion experientially, thereby offering a certain evidence for their assertion.

This situation is similar to that of the two seers of trees, the "cartesian" and the "druid"; both groups claim metaphysical certitude about what is seen. I shall call this initial certitude, *apodicticity*. To be apodictic means that I can return, again and again, to fulfill the experiential claim concerning seeing the drawing as hallway (or as pyramid).

Simplifying and reducing the example in this fashion may be burdensome to already enlightened people. Most likely, normal observers, already familiar with multi-stable configurations, have long since been able to see both variations alternatively. But viewers able to see either/both aspects are not at the same level of observation as our imaginary groups. They have ascended from the literal-mindedness of the first level by being able to see the alternation (of course, they see either one or the other aspect, but not both simultaneously). Their position, then, may be added as a second level of observational possibility. I shall term the group that sees either/both aspects Group A' (for ascendant).

EXPERIMENTAL PHENOMENOLOGY

Level I.	Noetic Context	Noema
Group H	literal-mindedness	hallway appearance
Group P	literal-mindedness	pyramid appearance
Level II.		
Group A'	polymorphic-mindedness	hallway and/or pyramid appearances

In spite of the obviousness of the polymorphic observation, several important preliminary points must be clarified even at this elementary level. First, observers of Group A' have exceeded the views of both H and P groups, at least in terms of relative comprehensiveness, since the ability to see both aspects is evidently superior to being able to see only one.

However, there is also an ascent in level. This ascent is indicated by two things that accompany ability to see alternatives. With the ascent in level, the viewer of alternatives does not lose apodicticity; he is able to return to both appearances and thus fulfill or verify the evidence of both. But the *significance* of that apodicticity changes. Once both aspects are possible, it is clear that neither the hallway nor the pyramid appearance can claim absoluteness or exhaustiveness for the possibilities of the thing.

To put this phenomenologically, the noema is now seen to contain two possibilities, and two possibilities as variations are relatively more *adequate* than one. The ascent in level is a move to (relative) *adequacy*, which now assumes a higher significance than mere apodicticity. However, it should not be forgotten that this relative adequacy is attained only through variations upon apodicticity. The fulfillability of the possibility must not be empty.

Simultaneously, the ascent in level also establishes a minimal *irreversible direction* for inquiry. This direction is non-transitive: once the ascent occurs, the observer cannot go back and recapture the naiveté of his previous literal-mindedness. While the variation upon both appearances can at any time be recaptured, the return to the claim that one, and only one, appearance is *the* appearance of the thing is now impossible. This change in the significance of apodicticity is permanent. The direction of inquiry looks thus:

Direction of Inquiry		Noetic Context	Noema	How Held
Level I.	H.	literal-mindedness	hallway	apodictic only
	P.	literal-mindedness	pyramid	apodictic only
Level II.	A'	polymorphic mindedness	hallway/ pyramid	apodictic and adequate

The direction of inquiry in which relative adequacy is more inclusive and yet retains the basic insights of the previous level can move from level I to level II, but once level II is attained, no simple reversion to level I is possible.

In the limited context of this example, in its general import, I am illustrating the first move of *epoché* and the phenomenological reductions. Husserl called for a move from the natural attitude, which is a kind of literal-mindedness imputing to things a presumed set way of being, to what he called the phenomenological attitude, here illustrated by polymorphic-mindedness. By its deliberate search for variations, the phenomenological attitude possibilizes phenomena as the first step towards getting at their genuine possibilities and the invariants inhabiting those possibilities. Potentially, the ascent to polymorphic-mindedness deliberately seeks a particular kind of *richness* within phenomena. But it also carries other implications. These may be seen if a further step-by-step discrimination of what is latent in the current example is undertaken.

Group A' has now discovered that the noema (the line drawing) contains two appearance possibilities. These are genuine apodictical possibilities of the figure. It may be said that they are *noematic* possibilities, inherent in the drawing. But all noematic possibilities are correlated with noetic acts. So far, only the context for those acts has been noted, that is, the type of beliefs surrounding the specific act which gives it its implicit metaphysical background. These beliefs are *sedimented*, and the viewer may or may not be able to abandon them.

In this context of "beliefs," each viewer saw the drawing *as* something, either as a hallway or as a pyramid. (It is important to note that in all cases, the viewers saw the configuration *as* something—they did not see a bare figure and then add some significance to it.) This seeing as_____was instantaneous. The noema appeared primitively as_____. The literal-minded viewers' first look was a naive look. They responded to what first came into view.

Such a response is typical of psychological experiments. Response times are usually limited, and the experiment is deliberately designed to eliminate reflection, critique or extensive observation. This raises the question what such an experiment reveals, an important question in our phenomenological inquiry. It is possible that an instantaneous glance shows us something basic about perception isolated from so-called higher- or lower-level conscious functions. It is equally possible that an instantaneous glance shows only what is most *sedimented* in the noetic context, the context within which perception occurs.

In both cases, the instantaneity of an initial glance must be noted with respect to the noetic act. A simple and often single noematic possibility occurs, which is correlated to the instantaneous glance. Such simplicity was noted earlier to be less than usual, since most viewers would see both alternatives within a very short time. In a psychological experiment with an increased response time, the subject sometimes reports that the figure spontaneously reversed itself. Such three-dimensional reversals are quite common, yet in the standard psychological literature, the noetic act is still noted as a relatively passive stare: If one looks at the figure long enough "it will reverse itself." If I had not broken down the situation into its phenomenologically ordered components, the standard accounts might seem sufficient.

Remaining within the limits of two noematic possibilities (hallway and/or pyramid) and within the limits of two noetic contexts (literal-mindedness or polymorphic-mindedness), it is possible to go one step further. If literal-mindedness occurs when an instantaneous glance is all that is allowed, and if initial polymorphic-mindedness is only characterized as a passive stare, what happens with a more *active* observation? This possibility is easily established by showing that the spontaneous reversal of the two appearance possibilities can occur *at will*.

The *free* variation is easily learned. Return to the hallway/pyramid figure and look at it; when one of its possibilities is fixed, blink your eyes (if necessary name the other possibility to yourself) and aim for its alternate. Within seconds, or at most minutes, you will find that each of the variations is easily attained at will. This kind of looking is a modification of polymorphic-mindedness. It opens the way to a further stage of the inquiry.

Suppose, now, the figure is presented again, only this time there is a third response from a group of people viewing the drawing. This new group, temporarily placed at the literal-minded level, claims the figure is neither a hallway nor a pyramid, but is a *headless robot*. See this appearance or noematic possibility by returning to the drawing and the guide picture:

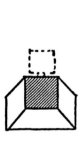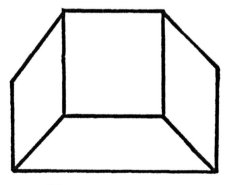

The robot has a body (the shaded area of the guide picture) and is lacking a head (the dotted outline in the guide picture). He needs to support himself with crutches (the outside vertical lines), which run from the ends of his arms (the upper diagonals) to the ground (the bottom horizontal). His legs are the lower diagonals.

Once this appearance or noematic possibility is grasped, fulfilled noetically, a rather dramatic transformation of the first two possibilities occurs. The three-dimensionality of both the hallway and the pyramid appearances is replaced by two dimensionality; the robot is seen to be flat and standing upright. This noematic possibility is quite distinct from both the others and stands on its own, if the pun can be allowed.

How are we to integrate this possibility with the previous situation? Theoretically, it is possible to take the third group of viewers, Group R (for Robot), as an equally naive group and put them on level I, which now looks like this:

Level I.	Noetic Context	Noema
Group H	literal-mindedness	hallway
Group P	literal-mindedness	pyramid
Group R	literal-mindedness	robot

But there is something irregular about this. Empirically, the instantaneous glances allowed in the usual experiments do not produce this third group, or, if it is produced, it is a rare variation.

There seems to be a relative weight or naturalness in the first two variations, which appear three dimensional, and not in the third, flat variation. Is it the case that in the first two variations, normal perceptual effects are being noted, while in the third something else is being shown? The question is whether an order of perception or an order of sedimentation is involved. This cannot be answered immediately, but a point can be made about the difference between the usual empirical psychology and a phenomenological psychology.

Multi-Stable Phenomena: A Phenomenological Deconstruction

Phenomenologically, the primary question concerns the structure of possibilities, the conditions for such and such empirical occurrences. Its first look is a look for possibilities and their limits, postponing any quick conclusions or generalizations from a straightforward empirical situation. Conversely, its investigation must be concrete, employing actual variations.

At the second level (polymorphic-mindedness), there also occurs a problem of integrating the robot-appearance with the previous situation. Once group A' viewers become aware of the robot appearance, they can add it to the series of variations along with the previous two variations. Group A' now has as its noematic possibilities: hallway and/or pyramid and/or robot. The direction of the inquiry—from apodicticity in each alternative to adequacy—has been maintained. (Once the third variation occurs and is established, one cannot go back to seeing the figure only as one of the three, without the changed significance of apodicticity occurring.)

This new modification of polymorphic-mindedness introduces a new variable and a new question. If what was taken to be *the* appearance of the noema has given way to two alternate appearances, and these have now given way to a third, has the range of noematic possibilities been exhausted? The discovery of a third possibility is not merely a modification of level II; rather, it introduces a new element.

The new element points to the inherent radicalism of variational method. The possibilization of a phenomenon *opens* it to its *topographical* structure. The noema is viewed in terms of an open range of possibilities and these are actively sought noetically. Thus, a special kind of viewing occurs, which looks for what is *not usually* seen. Nevertheless, what is seen is inherent in the given noema. This modification of polymorphic-mindedness is a new noetic context (open), corresponding to the possibilities of the noema (open). The significance of both noema and noesis has been modified.

Although it is possible to interpret this modification of polymorphic-mindedness as either an ascension to a new level or an intensification of the (already attained) ascendance to polymorphy, it certainly radicalizes ordinary viewing. This radicalization can be plotted on the diagram showing development of the method of inquiry as:

Level I.	Noetic Context	Noema
Group H	literal-mindedness	hallway
Group P	literal-mindedness	pyramid
Group R	literal-mindedness	robot
Level II.		
Group A'	polymorphic-mindedness	alternation hallway/pyramid (ordinary reversals)
Group A^m	polymorphic-mindedness (open possibility search)	alternation hallway/pyramid/ robot/?— (topographical possibilities)

Here the essential features of the direction of inquiry are preserved, but have been intensified. Group A^m (ascendant modified) has more alternations than Group A' (simple ascendant as opposed to any of the literal-minded groups). *Relative* adequacy is increased and is more comprehensive than in the ordinary alternation. Two certainties are preserved: first, all initial apodicticities are retained, in that they may be experientially recaptured; second, the direction of inquiry is certain, in that the attainment of relative adequacy is intuitively obvious, since each new alternation makes for more adequacy than the previous ones.

How far this procedure can go is not certain. Once alternatives are opened, only the actual investigation can show if closure is possible.

Multi-Stable Phenomena: A Phenomenological Deconstruction

Through the first example, I have illustrated the structure of a phenomenological inquiry, its logic of discovery. If, now, the potential attained at the modified level of Group A^m is read back into the lower stages of observation, one can begin to understand this procedure. The universal level of possibilization ("possibilities precede actualities in an eidetic science") includes, but transcends, all previous levels of the possible. It preserves the validity of each lower level in that it does not lose the ability to re-fulfill each experiential aim. At the same time, it has ascended to a higher level of sight, which transforms the significance of both thing and act of seeing. Suspending beliefs (naive noetic contexts) is needed to open the possibilities of the seen to their topographical features; otherwise the possibilities are confined to sedimented, ordinary viewing. The radicalized vision of modified polymorphy is not presuppositionless, as some have claimed; it is the attainment of a new and *open* noetic context. In Husserlian language, this attainment occurs in the switch from the natural attitude to the phenomenological attitude.

I have used the hallway example to reveal only the first steps of the essential shape of the phenomenological inquiry. I did not exhaust its possibilities, but though what follows might have been done in terms of this example, I shall turn to a series of similar multi-stable drawings and begin a more adequate and systematic deconstruction of their initial appearances in order, gradually, to approximate the topography inherent in the noema and the possibility search in a phenomenological noetic context.

Chapter Five

Variations upon Deconstruction: Possibilities and Topography

With the general shape of the inquiry determined, the hermeneutic rules of procedure introduced, and one example partially analyzed, it is possible to begin variations upon a group or class of structurally similar drawings. Once again, variational method is employed to open the phenomenon to its topographical features. Such viewing looks for what is potentially there in the noema. This instantaneous glance is far from naive immediacy. It is a view seeking possibilities as an expert investigator in a field study would look for subtle markings by which to distinguish the creatures he is observing.

For example, bird watching. The viewer notes the general configuration and silhouette of the bird and looks for minor markings, often very difficult to detect. Beginners seldom distinguish between the vast variety of sparrows, yet with visual education, they soon learn to detect the different markings of song, chipping, white-throated and other sparrows. The educated viewer does not create these markings because they are there to be discovered, but—in phenomenological language—he *constitutes* them. He recognizes and fulfills his perceptual intention and so sees the markings as meaningful. So, in what is to follow, vision is educated through a possibility search seeking the constitution of validly fulfillable variations. One aim is to arrive at a more adequate understanding of perception itself through this process.

Example Two: The Curved Line

The first drawing in this series is a very familiar one. The center lines are usually said to appear curved, whereas in reality they are straight and parallel. I call this the curved-line example.

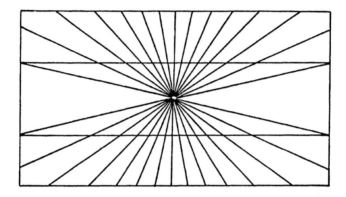

Suppose a situation similar to our previous example, i.e., a group of persons observing what appears in the above drawing. Some people view this as an optical illusion, the apparent curve of the central horizontal lines being interpreted as an effect of the configuration.

However, we will begin the noetic-noematic analysis with the preliminary oversimplified situation. One group of observers sees these lines as curved; they take this to be *the* appearance of the phenomenon, and can be identified in the same way as the initially naive groups of example one.

Level I.	Noetic context	Noema
Group C	literal-mindedness	curved lines

Seeing curved lines in the drawing is the normal way in which this configuration is taken in its ordinary noetic context or as sedimented in ordinary beliefs.

Furthermore this initial appearance seems natural, so much so, that a reversal does not spontaneously occur. In this example, too, certain appearance aspects seem to be privileged in normal ordinary perception. But this example is different from our first example, in that there is no reversal. Wherein, then, lies the possibility of alternate literal views or of a second level of viewing with either/both appearances?

Here we might introduce an artifice to demonstrate that the apparently curved lines are really straight. But, given our method's demand that every variation must be actually experienceable, a problem emerges. Take the following artifice:

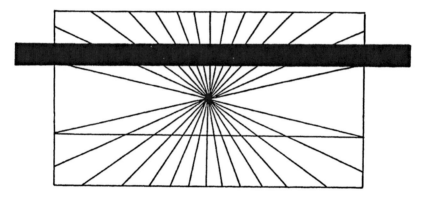

Here an external element has been added in the form of a measuring device laid over the original drawing. Now, noting the clear parallel between the ruler and the horizontal line in the drawing, it is possible to see that the line is not curved. But this is cheating, because it radically alters the original perceptual situation. A curved-line drawing without a ruler is not the same as a curved-line drawing with a ruler. So I shall discard the artifice. If alternate possibilities are to be shown as belonging to the noema, they must be discovered *within the drawing itself*. Return to the original drawing:

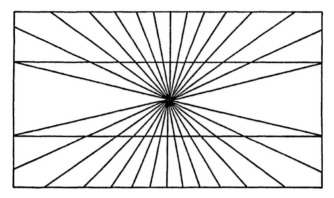

This time, look at the drawing in the following way: First, *focus* your gaze intently upon the vertex, where all the diagonal lines converge in the center of the figure. Second, deliberately see the vertex as three dimensional, and in the far distant background, that is, push the vertex back, as it were, until the diagonal lines are seen to lead to infinity. Granting that this takes a certain amount of concentration, subjects usually can do the task quickly, and then the formerly curved horizontal lines appear straight. But this is so only as long as the subject focuses upon the vertex intensely, making the horizontal lines peripheral to the central focus.

Although this kind of seeing seems artificial, we now note an alternative appearance to the drawing. Suppose that in the imaginary situation someone saw the curved-line figure first and simply as a three-dimensional distant vertex. Were that the case, we would immediately have an alternative.

Level I	Noetic Context	Noema
Group C	literal-mindedness	curved lines
Group S^f	literal-mindedness	straight lines (far apex)

Now we can compare the curved-line figure with the hallway figure, in that there is one flat appearance and one three-dimensional appearance.

Variations upon Deconstruction: Possibilities and Topography

In order to make the variations completely parallel to those of the hallway example, there would have to be a three-dimensional reversal possible. Return to the figure for a third time. Focus upon the vertex of the diagonal lines, but this time bring the vertex towards the very tip of your nose. That is, reverse (with effort if necessary) the direction of three-dimensionality. It may take more than one try to attain, but once you succeed note that the lines are straight when the focus is maintained upon the vertex of converging lines and the horizontal lines are peripheral.

There is a strict parallel of noematic possibilities with those of the hallway example: there are now two reversible three-dimensional appearances and one flat appearance. The direction and shape of a phenomenological inquiry occurs, with both levels, as it did in the hallway example.

Direction of Inquiry	Noetic Context	Noema
Level I		
Group C	literal-mindedness	curved lines
Group S^f	literal-mindedness	straight lines (far apex)
Group S^n	literal-mindedness	straight lines (near apex)
Level II		
Groups A' to A^m	polymorphic mindedness	curved/straight^f/ straight^r/?—^{n}

While the parallel of two three-dimensional and one two-dimensional possibilities is now demonstrated, there remains a curious difference between what occurred normally and what occurred with difficulty. In fact, in the curved-line example, the empirical order of discovery is the exact reverse of the hallway order. In the hallway example, the first appearances were three-dimensional and easily detected as reversible alternates; the flat, robot appearance came second and perhaps with a little initial resistance. In the curved-line example, the flat appearance with curved lines came first, while the reversible three-dimensional appearances came second and perhaps with difficulty.

Here the question of whether an order of perception or of sedimentation of beliefs determines the empirical order becomes even more enigmatic. To assert that this inversion of empirical order is perceptual, one would have to maintain that something in the figure naturally determines the order. If one asserts that the empirical order is only the result of sedimented noetic contexts, one would have to show how this order is arbitrary. Unless something appears that distinguishes the way in which the three-dimensional effect belongs inherently to the hallway and not to the curved lines, it is possible there is a tendency to arbitrariness to the empirical order of appearances. But it is clearly too early to conclude this is definitively so.

However, at the phenomenological level of the open search for the topography of the perceptual noema, correlated with the active looking of an open possibility search, it is now the case that the two examples display the same invariant structural features, allowing at least a three-dimensional reversal and a flat appearance, regardless of the empirical order of discovery. But note that something new has been introduced into the inquiry while it is underway. I described seeing the first example as (like)_____in terms of a kind of story. The drawing appeared as (like) a hallway, or as (like) a pyramid, or as (like) a headless robot. Once the appearance had been named, the observer could easily identify the noematic possibility. This story device, a metaphorical naming, connects the abstract figure with something familiar. The context of familiarity is such that the names are names of ordinary well-known things.

Suppose, when considering the hallway example, we found empirically that all the members of the hallway group were carpenters. They were accustomed to building hallways—in fact, that is almost all they ever did. In this case, the order of appearance would not be surprising at all. Plainly, carpenters who build hallways are likely to see the abstract drawing as something familiar. If we discovered that all those who saw the figure as a cut-off pyramid were pyramid builders, there would be no surprise about the order. At level one, the same goes for the robot group.

Of course, the story device is not neutral. It allows or suggests a certain way for the perceptual act to take shape. But it does so indirectly. One does not have to know what one is doing perceptually to have the appearance coalesce as a hallway or a pyramid or even a robot, once the appearance is recognized as such. One sees spontaneously, once the suggestion is made. This is not to say that the appearances could not have been discovered without names; a story device simply provides an easy and unselfconscious way for the appearances to be noted.

However, while a story device could have been used in the curved-line example, it would have been secondary. For the new element was a set of direct instructions about how to look: focus upon the vertex and then push the lines either forward or back, either toward infinity or to your nose. (As a passing observation, those who are highly successful in pushing the lines to infinity and back again, can learn to do this on a continuum, so that the horizontal lines may be seen to be straight, gradually curve and then restraighten.) Here, a direct connection can be made with a feature of both the visual field and the noetic act: a ratio between what is focal and what is fringe.

The direct instructions given to the viewer of the curved-line figure deliberately modify the normal or ordinary way the figure is initially taken. In a short glance resulting in the flat variation, the figure is taken as a whole, a totality. The entire figure appears within a wide focus. But under the instructions on how to see, that focus is modified to a narrow focus, with the results already noted.

Phenomenologically interpreted, this is to say that the way in which noetic shape (focusing) is modified, is a condition for the possibility of seeing certain shapes rather than other noematic appearances. Nor was this feature absent from the hallway example, though there the role of focus was indirect. In the hallway example,

I drew attention by the device of the guide picture, to a particular aspect of it: the central square. In both the hallway and the pyramid possibilities, this indirect focal act played its part. But when the headless robot figure occurred, there was a deliberate, although indirect, drawing of focus away from the central square. Mentioning the absent head, the arms and legs, and the ground on which the robot stood, provided a wide focus and so a flat configuration to the figure. The noetic act functioned to allow this different possibility to emerge.

Here we move towards resolving the question of whether perceptual or sedimented order controls the way in which empirical orderings occur, but the advance transforms the question. On the one hand, the empirical order clearly contains habitual sediments affecting how a particular configuration is taken. Yet on the other hand, in all appearances, a certain structural feature of perception is operative (in this case, focus—with the added possibility of three-dimensional effect).

For the moment, note two different strategies of interpretation within the investigation. The use of story devices and (metaphorical) naming I shall call a *hermeneutic* strategy. In a hermeneutic strategy, stories and names are used to create an immediate noetic context; they derive their power of suggestion from familiarity or from elements of ordinary experience. The story creates a condition that immediately sediments the perceptual possibility. In untheoretical contexts, this has long been used to let someone see something. Story tellers, myth makers, novelists, artists and poets have all used similar means to let something be seen. Plato, at the rise of classical philosophy, often paired a myth or fable with argument or dialectic. Within the context set by the story, experience takes shape.

But, note what happens in terms of the functions and structures of perception in the hermeneutic strategy: neither has to be known (theoretically) nor do directions about how to see occur. Instead, there is a gestalt-event. All at once, the desired effect is achieved; one sees it in an instant. And even if the shift from what was expected or ordinarily taken is dramatic and radically different, once it occurs it is so obvious that one wonders why it was not seen in that way before.

Ultimately, the hermeneutic strategy places its primary emphasis upon language. The symptomatic use of language as a story device illustrates the point. Perception takes shape within and from the power of suggestion of a language-game. It sees according to language. This strategy is the basis of what has become known as *hermeneutic phenomenology*. Historically, the preeminent figure working it out was Martin Heidegger, but Paul Ricoeur also took this direction.

Hermeneutic strategy tends to place its emphasis upon a noematic weighting, although in a somewhat unusual sense. The story lets something be seen; thus, what stands out is the noematic possibility. *How* this occurs, at least in terms of the mechanisms of perception, is less important than *that* it occurs or can occur in the ways open from the topography of the noema. In terms of another long tradition of philosophy, a hermeneutic strategy is more likely to be realist, insofar as it gives a certain precedence to the thereness of the noema. Language is the means, the primary relation, of the condition for the possibility of this discovery.

The second strategy I shall call a *transcendental* strategy. By this I mean, that like transcendental philosophy with its theme centering upon the subject, the way in which perception functions is made thematic. This is the counterpart to the hermeneutic strategy and can be seen to function with a certain *noetic* tendency.

The instructions on how to look, rely on a certain knowledge of the mechanisms of perception and on a turn to the subject as active perceiver. This noetic turn stresses the activity of viewing as the condition for the possibility of the object appearing as it does. In its most extreme form, particularly in the work of Edmund Husserl, its tendency is to emphasize the constitution of meaning done by the subject. In terms of the usual traditions of philosophy, this gives the transcendental strategy an idealist emphasis.

Transcendental strategy, however, is also analytic in its procedure. If one knows enough about the structures of perception, ideally, one should be able to deduce, or at least predict, which effects will eventually occur. One may guide viewing from the knowledge of its structural possibilities.

Yet both of these strategies, in spite of a tendency to emphasize one or the other of the correlational foci, point up the same phenomena and utilize variational method to achieve the ultimate understanding of invariance, limits and range of possibilities. In continuing the analysis of multi-stable examples, I shall utilize both strategies and attempt to demonstrate how a knowledge of invariants is built up in the process.

Chapter Six

Expanded Variations and
Phenomenological Reconstruction

The analysis of bi-morphic examples in the two previous chapters proved inadequate in their simplicity. The following analysis undertakes a further probing into the topography of similar drawings, with an eye to attaining greater and greater degrees of adequacy.

Example Three: The Cube Series

The following three instances of multi-stable phenomena consist of variations upon the well-known Necker cube. In the standard psychologies, this figure is usually said to reverse itself spontaneously in two three-dimensional appearances. If the cube is viewed (in ordinary, passive gazing) over a period of time, its three-dimensionality reverses itself.

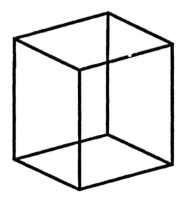

In .accordance with the already established phenomenological analysis, this reversal can be noted as two variations of polymorphy. (Since the examples in this chapter are polymorphic, the literal-minded characteristics of level one do not apply; for this reason, level one can be dispensed with for the remainder of this inquiry.) These two appearances are three-dimensional reversals of a cube. In this respect, the cube example displays an empirical order contiguous with the hallway example: at the polymorphic level, the noetic-noematic analysis shows one noematic possibility with a forward three-dimensional aspect, the other with a rearward aspect. In the diagram below, Cube^f symbolizes the forward aspect, Cube^r, the rearward.

Level II	**Noesis**	**Noema**
Polymorphy (A^m)	seeing as———►	Cube^f/Cube^r/? . . . . n

Here, the slight change in the diagram assumes that the polymorphic level has been established, and interest lies solely in the multiple possibilities. I also assume the observations to be active ones situated within the open noetic context of phenomenological inquiry. Empirically, the first appearances are two and have been arranged in the either/both alternative order.

Two further points concerning this stage of inquiry should be noted. First, the symbol, ? . . . . n, as used in the diagram, suggests an open search for greater and greater relative adequacy. An active search must be made for further possibilities: what noematic possibilities can the figure contain? Only after an adequate, or at least sufficient, number have been discovered can further claims be made about invariances and the topography of the phenomena. Here we have a problem—we do not know how far such possibilities extend—and a question—how do these possibilities arise?

Second, now that the noematic possibilities have been narrowed down to topographical possibilities (as yet open), the noesis must be similarly narrowed down. In the changed diagram the wider framework of the noetic context is presupposed, but now the specific structure of the noetic stance must also be clarified. Phenomenologically, this is done in correlation with the noematic possibility where the noesis is reflexively noted.

If I return to the figure and its reversal, I can note something about the transition. In the process of reversal, the figure seems to move. Giving way from its first stabilization to its second stabilization, it jumps, apparently in motion, before being fixed again. If there is a change in noematic aspect, can a correlation be noted noetically? According to the previous analysis, with respect to visual noema, there was a reflexive reference to the perspectival position of the viewer. Here the clue for noetic change is discovered.

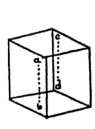 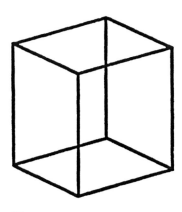

(The guide picture is inserted in order to identify key features.)

If I return to the reversal transition and query the perspectival position in the two appearances of the cube, I find that there is indeed a corresponding change. This can be put as a conditional (as if). In the guide picture, the most forward vertical line in its forward reversal appears to be line a-b. Noetically, the position of the viewer is as if he were somewhat above the figure, looking down at it. In the reversal, this noetic position shifts isomorphically with the shift in noematic appearance. In the rearward reversal, the most forward line is c-d, and the position of the viewer is as if the cube were being seen from below, the viewer looking up at it. This shift in noetic positions can be detected in the transition from one noematic possibility to the other. The isomorphism of noema-noesis in both its noematic appearance and the noetic position can be diagrammed correlatively:

Level II	Noesis	Noema
	seeing as (p^d)	Cube^f
Polymorphy	seeing as (p^u)	Cube^r
	? . . . . . n	? . . . . n

Here "p" stands for noetic position and "u" and "d" symbolize the upward or downward perspectives. Note that the downward perspective correlates with the forward and the upward with the rearward cube appearances: *I* look downward, or *I* look upward from my position.

Once this factor is noted reflexively, it is possible to refine the awareness of position as a guide to increasing *control* over the noematic appearances. For instance, to make the cube reverse itself rather than allow it spontaneously to reverse itself, I first see it in whichever three-dimensional appearance it shows itself, then I blink (perhaps saying to myself the name of its reversed appearance), and with a little practice, I soon get the variant I want. I can refine this practice by "placing myself" in position to see either the downward or upward and thus get the variant required. Furthermore, in this shift of position, I also change the central point of focus for the two variants. For the downward position of looking at the forward facing cube, I focus concentratedly at the point "a," whereas in the reversal, I shift the focus to point "c."

This development is clearly a kind of noetic training relying upon basically transcendental strategy which takes the shape of instructions on how to see. However, it is important to remain within the topographical limits of the phenomenon. The variations must be variations of the phenomenon and not visualized imaginative additions. They must be perceptual variants of the cube.

Noetically, three structural possibilities have been isolated: (a) the *ratio* of focus to fringe, which is controllable within the limits of vision, (b) the point of focus from which the field expands and shifts, and (c) a shift in relative position with respect to the noema. In each case there remains an isomorphism, a strict correlation, between noema and noesis. Only strategically the emphasis has been placed momentarily on the noetic side. However, this device accumulates clues that expand the search for significant variations within the topography of the multi-stable phenomenon.

Return again to the cube. At this point, two alternations have been noted; these appear in empirical order and have the same effect as the hallway example. If the cube displays the same topographical possibilities as the hallway, a flat appearance should also be found. But the sedimented recalcitrance of the natural attitude is complicated in this instance by two factors: the cube drawing is more complex and has more elements than the hallway; this complexity precludes easy and immediate identification with any ordinary object. This is not to say that a flat appearance is impossible to attain, only that empirically, the degree of recalcitrance in attaining flat variations is higher than that for the hallway figure (although its order remains the same).

If the noetic transcendental strategy is followed, there is one tactic for allowing the flat configuration to occur that should work. In the hallway and the curved-line examples, the flat or two-dimensional gestalt occurred with a widened unconcentrated focus. It should thus be possible to widen one's focus deliberately, avoiding concentration on any point in the figure, and attain a flat or two-dimensional appearance. With some effort, this succeeds, though stability is more difficult to maintain than with the two previous variations.

However, it is always more difficult to attain gestalts with the transcendental strategy of instructions on how to view than with the noematically oriented hermeneutic strategy. If a background story can be found to allow the third variation to appear, its stability will coalesce almost instantaneously. Suppose, now, that the cube drawing is not a cube at all, but is an insect in a hexagonal opening.

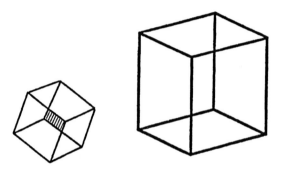

This view can be accomplished if the central parallelogram (shaded area in the guide picture) is seen as the insect's body, its six legs being the lines stretching to the sides of the hexagon (which may be a hole or whatever). Once again, the noematic gestalt emerges simply through the device of a story. The imaginative background leads perception into this possibility.

The cube example now shows the same topographical possibilities as the hallway and curved-line examples. Thus, an initial weak generalization can be made about the topographical features of all three drawings. The parallelism is indicated below, with the dimensional aspects symbolized as indicated, where 3-d^f means three-dimensional forward; 3-d^r, rearward and 2-d, two dimensional. The numbers in parentheses indicate the empirical order of seeing; (1) is first in empirical order of seeing, (2) is second.

Topographical Possibilities

Hallway	$3\text{-}d^f(1)/\ 3\text{-}d^r(1)/\ 2\text{-}d\ (2)$
Cube	$3\text{-}d^f(1)/\ 3\text{-}d^r(1)/\ 2\text{-}d\ (2)$
Curved line	$3\text{-}d^f(2)/\ 3\text{-}d^r(2)/\ 2\text{-}d\ (1)$

In terms of apriori possibilities, each figure shows the same topography, but in terms of empirical order with degrees of recalcitrance to deconstruction to pure topographical possibilities, the curved-line example's order is inverse to that of the hallway and cube (symbolized by the numbers in parentheses).

The demonstration establishing the same topographical possibilities is still not complete. Furthermore, the enigma of whether the recalcitrance of the empirical order of possibilities is due to sedimentation of habitual beliefs or to perceptual factors remains unresolved. Resolution calls for a still more radical phenomenological procedure.

The polymorphy discovered in the three examples is not adequate for a full descriptive analysis of topographical possibilities. Once more I return to the cube with a more radical intent and a more active search for topographical possibilities. These must be intentionally fulfillable to count as evidence in the accumulation of depth structures of multi-stable phenomena. I revert to the hermeneutic strategy:

 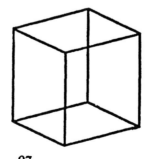

Suppose I tell you that the cube is not a cube at all, but is a very oddly cut gem. The central facet (the shaded area of the guide picture) is nearest you, and all the other facets are sloping downwards and away from it. Once this is seen (it may take a moment or two for the gestalt to occur), note what happens. First, a completely new three-dimensional appearance results, one not at all in keeping with the original three-dimensional appearance of the cube. Second, the significance of the various elements and lines in the drawing are rearranged with the new gestalt. The story has allowed a new configuration to be seen.

Now, suppose I tell you that the gem is also reversible and give a new story to let this be seen. Suppose you are now inside the gem, looking upwards, so that the central facet (the shaded area of the guide picture) is the one farthest away from you, and the oddly cut side facets are sloping down towards you. When this appearance occurs, there exists a fifth possibility for the cube example. Prior to further interpretation, the gain in topographical insight may be shown:

Topographical Possibilities

Cube $\quad$ 3-d^f $\quad$ /3-d^r $\quad$ /2-d $\quad$ /3-d$^{f'''}$ $\quad$ /3-d$^{r'''}$ $\quad$ /? . . . . n
(cube fore) (cube rear) (flat) (gem fore) (gem rear)

The polymorphy of the cube example is now more open than ever. Five possibilities have been discovered as genuine topographical possibilities of the drawing. The hermeneutic strategy has allowed noematic possibilities to be seen. Imaginary contexts permit easy gestalts to occur. Here a careful distinction should be made. The imaginary context is a background context. It does not add anything visual to the noematic possibility of the drawing in the sense of visually projecting something on the configuration. When such a visualistic, imaginary projection is done, it is clearly of quite a different order from continuing to treat the drawing as an open geometric configuration.

Expanded Variations and Phenomenological Reconstruction

If a visual and imaginary projection added color to the gem, it would be possible to *imagine* it as red or blue by adding that visual imaginary component. But that is not what the background context does. Rather, background context offers a shortcut to noematic gestalts by providing for a spatial arrangement to occur.

Once the fourth and fifth noematic possibilities have been exhibited, it is possible to parallel the hermeneutic device with its transcendental counterpart which emphasizes the noetic correlate. Noting, for the moment, only those structural features of perceptual change that occur noetically, it can be seen that there are subtle changes in focus between the cube as cube, and the cube as a gem. The core aspect of the gem appearance is the central facet. In the cube appearance, either point "a" or point "c" is central, or focus depends on positionality: the downward or upward. It is evident that a noetically controlled search parallels the imaginary, hermeneutic search. Instead of telling a story that allows the gestalt to appear, it might be possible to continue changing focal points, to scan and gaze at new configurations much more analytically than through hermeneutic devices. This process removes the latent suspicion that a hermeneutic device adds something to the figure, and it appeals to the abstract and geometric-minded. But such a noetic device is slower and harder to describe initially, and it has to be cast in a tight technical language presupposing substantial understanding of perceptual structures.

This variation upon the two phenomenological strategies indirectly points the way in which most of these discoveries have occurred. It has been observed that creative discoveries are often first cast in metaphorical terms and that soft logics precede hard logics. Here, a repeated generation of initial noematic discovery through hermeneutic devices with later reflexive gains in the transcendental mode, is significant.

Regardless of which strategy is used in the expansion of polymorphy through a more radical phenomenological investigation, the direction of inquiry remains open with respect to adequacy. In moving step by step, it is advisable to consolidate gains, particularly as long as the empirical order is felt to conflict with the apriori order of topographical possibilities.

In the standard psychologies, a variation of the Necker cube is frequently used as the second example of a cube appearance:

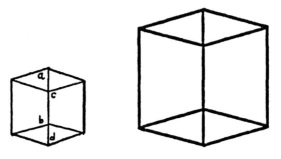

Without much effort, particularly in the light of what is beginning to be a re-sedimentation of noetic context, it is possible to duplicate the initial variations simply:

> Variation 1: The new cube is seen to be facing forward with its three-dimensional effect seen from above, paralleling the former cube appearance, 3-d^f. (Line a-b is forward as in the guide picture.)
>
> Variation 2: A reversal of the above (line c-d in guide picture forward), 3-d^r.
>
> Variation 3: A two-dimensional appearance which is usually somewhat easier to see with this drawing than with the previous one.

Although three variations upon the drawing is one more than most standard psychologies admit, phenomenologically it should be suspected that at least two more variations are possible, as with the first cube drawing.

Briefly resorting to the story device, it is relatively simple to establish variations four and five. In variation four, suppose you are lying flat on your back, looking upward at the underside of a small, medieval church ceiling. The ridge of the ceiling (line c-b in the guide picture) is farthest from you, the sides slope down toward you as if to meet upright walls. This is variation $3\text{-}d^{r'}$. A reversal of this new and quite different three-dimensional appearance is possible. Suppose you are now above the church, looking down on the roof. The ridge of the roof (line c-b) is central and nearest your position, the sides now slope downward, away from your position. This establishes variation $3\text{-}d^{f'}$.

The five variations noted for the first cube drawing are now established for the second cube drawing:

Topographical Possibilities

$$\text{Cube}^2 \qquad 3\text{-}d^{f'}/3\text{-}d^{r'}/2\text{-}d/3\text{-}d^{f''}/3\text{-}d^{r''}/? \ldots \text{n}$$

If my step by step examples have been followed carefully, it should be getting easier to see alternatives. Phenomenologically interpreted, this education of vision suggests that the usual recalcitrance of a sedimented noetic context is loosening.

Experiencing a certain loosening of ordinary expectations, the viewer begins to suspect that all abstract drawings (insofar as they belong to this type) are more polymorphic than they are usually taken to be. Noematically, polymorphy is far more open to multiple stabilities than the naive first glance, which gives only one or two, or even three possible stabilities. This new ease of deconstruction may be shown by a rapid demonstration of a third cube drawing which also is frequently seen in standard psychologies.

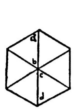 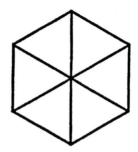

In the above figure, an initial empirical order different from the other cube drawings is likely. Its flat, two-dimensional appearance (i.e., as a hexagon) is likely to be seen first. In fact, the naive viewer might not even suspect it to be a cube if it were not deliberately placed in a series of cube drawings. Here again, sedimentation shows itself as the noetic context of the possibilities of appearance. What first appears does so in terms of familiarity and expectation within ordinary experience.

In order to vary empirical order, suppose the flat appearance occurs first. I shall elicit variations 3-$d^{f''}$ and 3-$d^{r''}$ prior to the cube appearances. The first non-cube three-dimensional appearance will occur if you suppose you are lying on your back, looking upward, inside a teepee. The intersection of the lines is the top where the teepee poles cross, and the sides are slanting down towards you on the ground. The reversal occurs when you suppose you are above the teepee, as if in a helicopter, looking down at it. Now the sides are slanted downwards from the intersection.

The empirical order in this case has developed as 2-d/3-$d^{r''}$/3-$d^{f''}$, which is quite different from that established in the other examples. It is obvious by now that this example has no natural order. Indeed, once these three variations on cube³ have been constituted, it is momentarily difficult to see cube³ as a cube (the first empirical appearances for cube¹ and cube²). But minor recalcitrance is not the same as impossibility. To constitute variations 3-$d^{f'}$ and 3-$d^{r'}$ you must intend a cube. To obtain the 3-d appearance in the forward-facing variation, focus on line a-b, as nearest you. This constitutes 3-d^{f}

with an upward angle. To obtain the reverse, shift your apparent position and look downward, the line c-d marking the near angle facing you.

The order in which the five variations on cube^3 occurred is:

Topographical Possibilities

Cube^3 2-d/3-d$^{r''}$/3-d$^{f''}$/3-d$^{f'}$/ 3-d$^{r'}$ / ?. . . . n

Clearly, however, this order was not a necessity and it could have been established differently.

Unless the hexagonal-type drawing is introduced in the cube series as below, its cube appearances are not intuitively obvious to naive experience.

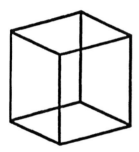 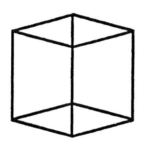 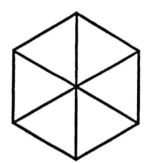

The series itself sets an initial context. Taking them initially as variations upon a cube, it is possible to go through the three-dimensional reversals in each of the drawings quickly. But it is increasingly likely that the empirical order is set by the sedimentation of an initial context.

We gain advantages from this conclusion: the role of context and sedimentation is increasingly isolated and its functions are observed. The phenomenological deconstruction which throws doubt upon the primacy of empirical order achieves two results. The role of context and sedimentation emerges as a possible theme for investigation; the gradual constitution of topographical possibilities frees the noema to assume its full richness and complexity.

Once these two regions (often confused in standard psychologies) are freed, it is possible to thematize each separately. Thematization is a reconstruction along phenomenological lines, in each case driving toward the structure of possibilities. On the side of the topography of the noema, subsequent phenomenological analysis deals with the range, structure and horizons of possible variations within the open context of phenomenological viewing. Here the aim is to isolate and describe the structural properties of the class of multi-stable phenomena. On the other side, not yet as thoroughly thematized, it is possible to envision a set of investigations into sedimented contexts as a related region of inquiry.

While the topography of the multi-stable phenomenon and the structure and function of the immediate context have not been exhausted, phenomenological deconstruction and the opening to a reconstruction within the limits of the phenomenon are significant steps beyond the initial situation with which the inquiry began. The objects of the inquiry—multi-stable phenomena—should appear in different ways to the now educated vision.

Compare the initial situation of vision with its current state, presuming that the exercises have been followed and fulfilled as indicated in each step. If the phenomenological education of vision has occurred, as it should, the following may be considered as relevant conclusions:

I. Initially, the phenomena (the drawings I have shown) appeared in one or two variations. This is always the case with most naive viewers, but interestingly, it is also the case with most standard psychologies.[1] In the psychologies, multi-stability is usually interpreted to be a bi-morphic phenomenon and it is assumed that this is all the phenomenon contains. If a third variation is pointed out, it is usually regarded as odd or weaker in stability than the normal bi-morphic reversal.

Contrastingly, within the purview of the phenomenological deconstruction with its concentration upon topographic possibilities, it is now seen that at least five possibilities may be obtained, and that once cleared from their initial sedimentations, these variations can be stabilized, easily attained and repeated.

This opening of the possible significance of the phenomenon is the result of *epoché* and the phenomenological reductions, which deliberately put aside ordinary assumptions and sediments—do violence to them, as it were—in order to free the phenomenon for its essential, rather than accidental, appearances. In ordinary and even standard psychological viewing, topographical possibilities do not show themselves spontaneously apart from the immediate and larger background noetic contexts. *Epoché* displaces that natural attitude or already sedimented context from the outset.

In ordinary and standard psychological views, a topographical possibility either does not show itself at all (I am not aware of any development of topography in the literature of psychology along the lines developed here), or it is discovered accidentally and usually dismissed.[2] Yet the implications of polymorphy are extremely important for both empirical and epistemological studies.

II. Once the phenomenon has been opened to a topographical investigation and its potential wealth discovered, a series of second-order gains may be discerned as well. The *eidetic* level is reached, and deeper layers of the invariants may be seen in the phenomenon. For example, it is evident, that all multi-stable drawings of the type being investigated should display more than one or two variants, and that something structural in polymorphy allows this multiplicity.

This leads to a second-order deconstruction of presuppositions about perception and the sedimented context. For example, the farther the investigator goes with the examination of multi-stable phenomena, the more likely it is that he will discover ever more quickly and easily a whole range of topographical possibilities in subsequent drawings. At the least, this shift from ordinary to open noetic contexts ruins the phenomenological investigator as a naive subject. For every group of phenomena being interrogated, ascendance to the open context is irreversible. In addition, it becomes more and more apparent that the empirical order depends on the way ordinary or common sense contexts are sedimented, rather than on perceptual structure, as such. In fact, once expectation of polymorphy is thoroughly consolidated, any variation in a multi-stable drawing can occur first.

This is not yet apparent in most standard psychological theories. People whose viewpoint is based on ordinary experience and certain theoretical commitments are reluctant to give up long-held expectations and assumptions. In discussing this material with psychologists, I have learned to predict a progressive reticence about the tenacity of sedimented theoretical views. It is usually a relatively simple matter to show that the phenomenon displays the perceptual possibilities demonstrated; once experientially verified, the phenomenon cannot be denied (apodicticity). But the implication of polymorphy is not often so quickly grasped. In the progressive reluctance to put aside assumptions, it is usually held that only the first one, two, or at most, three variations belong naturally to the phenomenon. All others are odd, or the constructions of an overactive imagination.

Yet neither of these viewpoints can hold. With practice, the odd ones become less odd, and each variation attains full stability and naturalness in a very short time. The order of appearance-variations becomes increasingly arbitrary. Experiential intuition itself is changing; as it does so, the sense of what is natural and of what is given also changes. Of course, in an empirical study using naive subjects (viewers who are not phenomenologically trained) with the usual experimental controls, only one or two variations will be noted. But this is to be expected, precisely because the ordinary viewer holds to a certain noetic context. Indeed, this background context is itself gradually being explicated in the process of this investigation.

Furthermore, the significance of the empirical study must be reinterpreted from the phenomenological point of view. If an instant glance, coupled with a strongly held but naive, ordinary noetic context, responds to the expected first appearance only, it is evidence of current sediment shape, rather than evidence of a primary characteristic of perception. While not denying the importance of empirical studies, phenomenologists must consider unacceptable those claims whose premise is limited by the present definition of empirical evidence. Phenomenologically, the structures of perception are more likely to be discovered through variational method, which investigates the whole range of possibilities from those of ordinary sediments to the most extreme horizontal possibilities.

Additionally, holding that odd cases are imaginative constructions does not protect the standard psychologies or ordinary experience from the potential loosening of long-held assumptions in the phenomenological experiment. Such imaginary backgrounds always relate to what is seen. To call the configurations in the cube series "cubes" is already to have named them. A named geometrical figure is as much an imaginary concept as the named insect figure that allowed the two-dimensionality of the cube to appear. Perception does not occur apart from language, and it is just as possible for names to lead experience as it is for experience to arrive at names. And if one follows the longer, indirect route of transcendental strategy, which instructs one how (and not what) to see, one arrives at the same effects, albeit tediously and painfully, without any hint of imaginary construction. The possibilities of polymorphy are the topographical possibilities of the thing itself as an open noema.

III. At this point in our discussion of *how* we see *what* we see, a substantial sense of change in our perception of the way things may be seen should have occurred. The ordinary viewer allows things to be seen in the sedimented context of ordinary beliefs. Because we are culturally familiar, not only with cubes, but also with drawings of cubes, the cube example appears first as a cube. The standard psychologies themselves are part of the belief-furniture of our ordinary universe.

Phenomenological observations do violence to the passivity of ordinary viewing. There is a deliberate probing of the phenomenon for something that does not at first show itself, and a growing sense of control over what is seen. This control has two aspects: one, it is able to elicit from the phenomenon what was not at first seen, and two, it obtains exactly the variations demanded in the order demanded. In the process, a new type of familiarity is constructed, the familiarity of polymorphy. There is a playfulness here akin to the playfulness found in artistic contexts. However, the free variations of the artist are given systematic and scientific purpose in the investigation of essential features and limits of a given phenomenal region.

In each of these three conclusions, we may speak of an ascent to the phenomenological attitude. If consolidated, this ascent is no longer a theoretical device, but becomes a permanent part of our conceptual machinery. Late in his career, Husserl noted precisely this: "It is to be noted also that the present, the 'transcendental' *epoché* is meant, of course, as a habitual attitude which we resolve to take up once and for all. Thus it is by no means a temporary act which remains incidental and isolated in its various repetitions."[3]

Notes

1. Many studies have been done on Necker cube reversals. This literature reveals that the implicit assumptions of the researchers have not gone beyond those of their subjects. It tacitly assumes that the odd reversibility of the cube is what is unique about the cube. One study noted that some subjects experienced a flat percept, but explicitly reports it as a hang-up associated with fatigue (the Morris article below, p. 236). See, for representative work, the following three studies in *Perceptual and Motor Skills*: (a) Frank Haronian and A. Arthur Sugarman, "Field Independence and Resistance to Reversal of Perspective," Vol. 22, 1966, pp. 543–546; (b) Helen A. Heath, Dan Erlich, and J. Orbach, "Reversibility of the Necker Cube: Effects of Various Activating Conditions," Vol. 17, 1963, pp. 539–546; and (c) B. B. Morris, "Effects of Order and Trial on Necker Cube Reversals Under Free and Resistive Instructions," Vol. 33, 1971, pp. 235–240.

2. Fred Attneave has discovered limited instances of what he calls "tristable" occurrences, but these are not expanded upon topographically. Fred Attneave, "Multistability in Perception," *Scientific American*, Vol. 225, Dec. 1971, p. 63.

3. Edmund Husserl, *The Crisis*, p. 150.

Chapter Seven

Horizons: Adequacy and Invariance

The phenomenological ascent, it should be evident, transforms both the sense of what is given and the understanding of how experience occurs. In ordinary experience a certain inflexibility is assumed to belong to givenness; a hallway and a cube appear naturally and obviously as what they are empirically taken to be. This is considered a *fact*-stratum concerning things and constitutes the naive sense of givenness. After phenomenological deconstruction, givenness is loosened so that the empirical order shows itself to be a result of an unstated context of beliefs. This movement from naivete to openness, increases with ever expanded adequacy over what is merely apodictic. Topographical possibilities replace the initial *fact*-stratum with an *essence*-stratum. All occurrences that exemplify facts take their place as variations upon an essential insight.

This is not to say that all givenness disappears, but that the significance of the given is transformed. Givenness in its phenomenological context becomes what is fulfillable. This is what is meant in Husserlian language by an experiential intuition. Any intentional aim that can be fulfilled is intuitively evident. (This language comes from

Husserl's mathematical background; he carried it over into phenomenology.) The fulfillability of facts remains possible at both the given and the intentional level, with the changed significance noted. Thus, the experiments we have been conducting can be called intuitional demonstrations. The type of intuition involved is similar to logical or mathematical intuition in terms of what is usually called self-evidence. Once a variation is seen, there can be no doubt that it has been seen, and its strength is like that of logical insight, but this time, in the region of perceptual experience. It is in this sense that phenomenology claims to be an essential or apriori science.

The fulfillability of the series of intuitional demonstrations is what remains as the core sense of givenness after the phenomenological deconstruction of what is first taken to be the case in ordinary experience. At the same time, this direction of ascent, which becomes operational for continued variations, drives toward an adequate understanding of the phenomena. However, the phenomenological level of operation is faced with a problem quite different from that of the empirical level, in that openness rather than facticity becomes problematic. The problem with open adequacy can be illustrated by following one more multi-stable example through a series of variations. I shall call this the circle example.

The Circle Example

The expectation that this figure will yield a series of variations is now part of a phenomenologically sedimented noetic context. But until the variations are performed and made intuitively evident, it is unclear how many and of what type they may be. Since empirical order has been largely replaced by an apriori order, it may be interesting to generate variations arbitrarily, making a parallel with the cube examples.

In the previous examples, the order appeared as first three-dimensional (easy), and then two-dimensional (initially more difficult), variations, symbolized as $3\text{-}d^f/3\text{-}d^r/2\text{-}d$. . . . Suppose these varia-

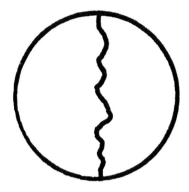

tions are to be displayed by the circle example. Initially, utilizing the hermeneutic strategy, the 3-d^f appearance can be seen as a giant clam standing on edge. The circle is a clam. The squiggled line is its mouth, which is curved and facing the viewer. The sides of the shell curve around from the mouth. This gives a three-dimensional forward-facing variation.

Once three-dimensionality is seen, its reversal is possible. Suppose you are inside the clam, looking at its mouth from the inside. The mouth makes a convex curve, farthest from you at the center and nearest where it meets the circumference of the circle; thus 3-d^r. Two-dimensionality is simple in this drawing, since the figure might as well be a circle with a squiggled line through it. If you like, it is a wire mobile hanging from the ceiling with a squiggled wire running through the middle. Here the order parallels that seen in the cube examples: 3-d^f/3-d^r/2-d/ / . . . . n.

Other variations are possible for an arbitrary order, for example, variation four is similar to the Janus-faced appearances of duck-rabbits and the Peter-Paul Goblet in which a figure/ground reversal occurs. For this variation, see the circle as a bi-morphic cameo. The left-hand side of the circle is the face of the cameo, while the right-hand side is the background. I shall symbolize this variation as 2-d^{dr} (dr for dominant right). Variation five is the reversal, the right-hand side being the face and the left-hand side being the background. This may be symbolized as 2-d^{dl} (dl for dominant left). At this point there are now five variations, three of which are two-dimensional variations:

Topographical Possibilities

Circle   3-d^f/3-d^r/2-d/2-d^{dr}/2-d^{dl}/ ? . . . . . n

There are now five variations, though without a strict parallel with the cube, since there are two three-dimensional and three two-dimensional variations. The two-dimensional variations, however, suggest that several noetic possibilities are active. Shift, then, to a noetic emphasis for a moment, and take note of these. The circle figure is clearly open to plays upon dominance and recessiveness, such as are already well known as figure/ground reversals in Gestalt psychology. Supposing a purely topographical projection, it should be possible to combine two noetic possibilities—figure/ground pos-

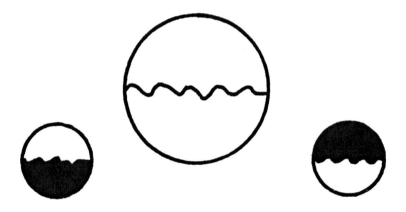

sibilities and three-dimensional possibilities—to constitute even more perceptual variants.

To make this point simply, I revert to the hermeneutic strategy

112

(stories). I shall also temporarily employ guide pictures and the device of turning the figure on its axis. But neither of these external devices are necessary, except for convenience, simplicity and directness.

In the next variations, dominance, recessiveness and three-dimensional effects are combined. Suppose you are looking through the periscope of a submarine. On the horizon (in the ordinary, not phenomenological, sense), the ocean (the shaded area in the left-hand guide picture) is dominant, with the sky above, recessive and open. Here the circle is the hole close to your eyes, through which you peer, while the ocean is more distant and the sky more distant yet. I shall symbolize this sixth variant as 3-d$^{d-r'}$ (d-r' for dominance-recessive prime).

An inversion of variation six is possible. Suppose you are looking into a cave through its opening. The dominant upper half of the circle (right-hand guide picture) is the foreground, and consists of stalactites hanging from the roof of the cave; the bottom, recessive half is the floor of the cave, which continues into the distance. Variation seven may be symbolized as 3-d $^{r-d'}$ (recessive and dominance reversed).

Nor do seven variations exhaust the intuitable possibilities of the circle example. When this example is used in classrooms at this juncture in teaching variational method, ten to fourteen variations are discovered by the students who have grasped the principle of topographical possibilities. Most of these, of course, are further variations upon the elements already noted.

Such variations may be predicted and fulfilled easily if the insight into the topographically essential traits of multi-stable figures has been grasped. For instance, variations upon three-dimensionality are made by projecting from the known elements toward those not yet known, and fulfillments attempted accordingly. In variations six and seven, there were three focal planes or main projected elements of the drawing. This may be illustrated by turning the viewing situation sideways and noting how a projection occurs:

113

FOCAL PLANES

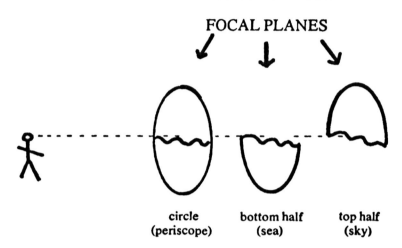

| circle | bottom half | top half |
| (periscope) | (sea) | (sky) |

This configuration interprets variation six, $3\text{-}d^{d-r}$. It is possible now, to project other possibilities according to where the elements of the drawing occur on all possible focal planes.

In a three-dimensional variation on the cameo variations, $2\text{-}d^{dr}$ and $2\text{-}d^{dl}$, it is possible to move one focal plane element of the drawing to coincide with the focal plane of the circle itself, leaving the other open and thus distant in nuanced appearance, as diagrammed below:

FOCAL PLANES

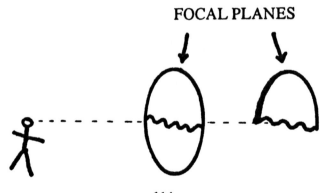

Its reversed appearance may also occur if the distant projected upper half replaces the bottom half which rests within the circle as in the diagram. (Such variations would be eight and nine, respectively, and stories may be found to allow these variations to coalesce. For instance, suppose you are looking through a ship's porthole with a smudge obstructing the lower portion of the porthole. Then only the upper half is open to the outside and that outside is projected in the infinite distance, etc.) Each of these variations can be experientially fulfilled and have their own apodicticity.

It is clear now that a large number of topographical possibilities occur within the noema of a multi-stable drawing. Furthermore, if the essential insight into the types of multiple variations in such drawings has been attained, many more variations can be found in the previous figures as well. At this stage, students in the classroom are able to discern from two to four more variants on the Necker cube.

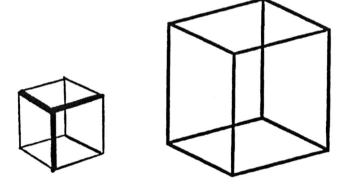

If, for example, the cube is seen, not as a cube but as a hexagon, with two sets of intersecting lines drawn inside it, one set superimposed upon the other, it appears either as flat, with one set of intersecting lines dominant and the other set recessive (as in the heavier lines of the guide picture), or it appears as weakly three-dimensional with one set of intersecting lines in front of the other (with reversals of dominant and recessive lines, and near and far lines, in the shallow three-dimensionality). The drawing and guide pictures above emphasize these features and should allow the variations to be seen.

Nor do these variations exhaust the cube's possibilities. However, two observations are now appropriate. First, the new variations are not as dramatic or as distinctive as the more obvious ordinary variations discovered earlier. The drama of discrimination has begun to take on a different tone. Once broken open, the ordinary sediment serving as the noetic background for vision recedes in significance as the extent of variations becomes known. The new appearance possibilities of multi-stable phenomena, at first strained and strange, become familiar and expected. I, for one, would be very surprised if I were not able to find polymorphy in a figure of this type that I had not yet investigated. Part of the secret of polymorphy has been penetrated, and so the subsequent variations become part of the work of refining what has already been attained in principle.

Second, as the extent of discernible variations is known, perceptual possibilities show themselves to be closer to conceptual, mathematical and logical possibilities than has been thought. Once the elements of perceptual possibilities are identified, we can do something like a deduction of what will and what will not be fulfilled within perceptual experience. A process like this was implicit in the circle example described. If the perceptual possibilities of dominance and recessiveness (figure/ground relations) can be combined with the projective possibilities of three-dimensionality, then we should be able to make an indefinite number of discriminations within abstract multi-stable drawings.

We now know that the field of perceptual possibilities is vast and complex, yet there is a structure and ordering principle to it. Thus a new set of essential conditions emerges simultaneously with the breaking of the naive stereotype for multi-stable figures.

I shall not here elaborate all these conditions. Several have been alluded to in the last few pages. Noematically, for example, multi-stable figures contain possibilities for multiple arrangements of figure and ground, dominance and recessiveness, with respect to any given number of elements displayed. These elements may be projected in an indefinite number of possible arrangements with respect to the projective possibilities of nearness and distance in apparent three-dimensionality. Merely by combining such noematic traits, it becomes obvious that the number of possible combinations is large.

This is not to say that any conceivable combination is perceptually possible. The range of conceivability is probably much wider than that of perceptual possibility, even though the range of perceptual possibility is much more fluid and complex than ordinarily supposed. There are noetic limitations to perception, which derive from our finite bodily positions. For example, one noetic factor previously alluded to was the role of focus. Changing from wide focus to narrow focus can cause noematic changes (recall the curved-line example). Focusing on one part of a drawing can cause all the parts to arrange themselves around the area of focus and give a new and different appearance (this was part of the noetic device employed to turn the Necker cube into a two-dimensional insect). If this were a text in phenomenological psychology, it would elaborate these noematic and noetic features exhaustively and thus order the entire region of multi-stable perception.

It remains important to note that the explosion of the previously taken-for-granted phenomenon is nevertheless a contained explosion. The ordering process points to the limits of the phenomenon, the horizon of the multi-stable field. Horizons are by their nature indefinite and at the farthest extreme from what is clear and distinct, but they remain at least indistinctly discriminable.

A clue to the noematic horizon of the figures may be obtained from the relevance or irrelevance of the hermeneutic stories. Not just any story will do, nor will any empty possibility be fulfilled by looking at the figure. The hallway example does not let itself be seen as a swan flying. Only stories that free possibilities hidden in the configuration allow the gestalts to appear. Whatever the extent of the fulfillable variations may be, they remain dependent upon the *internal horizon* or limits that the drawing contains.

This horizon is a clue from which the structures of perception are reflexively learned. Corresponding to the relevance or irrelevance of the hermeneutic device is the structural limitation of perception. For example, the act of focus is extremely important in allowing a figure to appear as such and such a possibility. The psychologist, Necker, noted early that a shift of what he termed a point of fixation causes the cube to reverse its initial three-dimensionality.

The focus not only fixes some point, facet or aspect of the drawing; it also serves as a value around which the other parts, facets or aspects are arranged. Yet while focus has flexible and expandable variations, it does not have infinite variations, for two reasons. It is difficult, if not impossible, to focus on two widely separated facets equally and at the same time, which suggests something like a perceptual law of the excluded middle. And when focus takes in the entire visual field, everything in the field becomes less distinct and more distant (look into the distance and widen your focus to note this phenomenon).

This latter feature of perceptual activity may be taken as a sign of the directedness of intentionality in its full phenomenological sense. But before considering the significance of directedness of intentionality to the future development of phenomenological investigation, it is necessary to reflect on the process of inquiry that has taken place with the extremely limited set of phenomena examined in this book.

Summary: A Reflection Upon the Inquiry

The foregoing pages have offered an introduction to some of the tribal language of phenomenology and a preliminary working out of one set of limited examples to show the style of investigation and point up its implications for subsequent phenomenological investigations. No claim is made, even for the simplified and limited examples of multi-stable drawings, to either exhaustiveness or complete adequacy. Rather, I have tried to illustrate how one does phenomenology. A brief recapitulation of the stages of the inquiry will show the development of this method in capsule form before we extrapolate its significance for more complicated and profound investigations.

The investigation has been purposely cast in a Husserlian guise. This is appropriate for several reasons: Edmund Husserl was clearly the founder and originator of the method that became phenomenology, almost all major work done by the great phenomenologists has been inspired by Husserl, and it is my own conviction that while Husserl cannot have the last word about phenomenology, he must have the first word. The analytic mind at work in the Husserlian style of phenomenology must inform all phenomenological study and distinguish between phenomenology proper, hard-headed phenomenology if you like, from soft-headed imitators. Husserlian phenomenology moves step by step, makes fine distinctions, and solidifies each item before moving on to the next development.

All these attributes are not only in keeping with the dominant spirit of twentieth-century philosophy, but are also necessary if philosophy is to retain a rigor parallel to that of the sciences. Taking a single small region of multi-stable perceptual phenomena, I have outlined some of the major elements in a descriptive (and phenomenological) psychology—all of which can be seen to lead to even finer and more microanalytic investigations.

This is not to say that a step-by-step process does not become orchestrated into a recognizable movement. If we reflect on what happened over the span of examples investigated, the larger movement can be seen.

Take note of the more dramatic features of the phenomenological shift.

(1) The first shift was what the Husserlian would call the deliberate shift from the natural to a phenomenological attitude. Those first

given appearances of the examples used, seemed to have a certain familiarity, a naturalness, which was taken for granted and tacitly assumed to be *the* possibility of the thing in question.

On reflection, the Husserlian *epoché* is a device for breaking the bonds of familiarity we have with things, in order to see those things anew. But it is a device, because Husserlian phenomenological seeing has already placed itself outside and above naive seeing.

(2) Phenomenological seeing deliberately looked for possibilities rather than the familiar, the taken for granted or the natural givenness of an object. Guided by this heuristic principle, phenomenological seeing pointed out strange possibilities—strange, that is, from the point of view of the sedimented and strongly held natural attitude. The first distinct perceptual possibilities appeared as dramatically different, surprising, and in some cases perhaps initially difficult to attain. This break with sedimented visual beliefs was necessary to clear the field for phenomenological, in contrast to empirical, investigation.

(3) Once broken, the visual beliefs were reshaped so that a new level of familiarity emerged, the level of essential seeing, or eidetic investigation in Husserlian language. Now the sense of phenomena was opened, and their possibilities seen to be multiple, complex and perhaps indefinite—limited only by the configurational internal horizons of each geometrical drawing. The sense of the phenomena changed, and the sense of seeing changed, both being open textured.

The diagram shows what is experienced in the change. The movement is a paradigm shift, which moves the investigator from one set of concerns, beliefs and habits of seeing to another. It also contains a value claim that the new paradigm is better than the familiar one, at least theoretically and philosophically, because (a) new discoveries are made, (b) the previous point of view is shown to be inadequate in perceiving its field of phenomena and in its theoretical insights, and (c) it allows the development of a depth ordering of the new wider field of phenomena.

The diagram of this larger movement is:

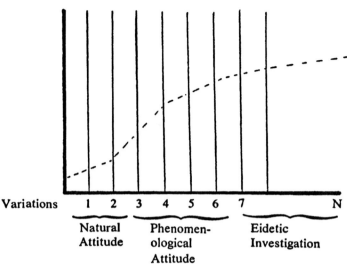

Horizons: Adequacy and Invariance

Variations   1   2   3   4   5   6   7   N

Natural   Phenomen-   Eidetic
Attitude   ological   Investigation
          Attitude

We have seen initially dramatic differences and distinctions discovered within the phenomena become a new, familiar (yet open)
field for the development of distinctions and differences. If this
movement was followed and consolidated, it becomes possible to
repeat the process with every multi-stable configuration. The new
expectations (noetic context) are that the drawing contains
n. . . . possibilities, and these may be actively sought out or elicit-
ed by the hermeneutic or the transcendental device. And while
sometimes drawings will still display the standard empirical order,
due to recalcitrant familiarity, increasingly, an arbitrary, although
essential, order will replace it. Let each try for himself.

Chapter Eight

Projection: Expanding Phenomenology

The simple and abstract examples I have employed in this book pose two difficulties for the extrapolation of phenomenological method into weightier problems. One comes in part from the simplicity of the examples. They are reduced phenomena, nothing but bare lines on blank backgrounds. And although even these simple phenomena turn out to be far more complex than they are usually taken to be, they are almost too suggestive. Once the natural attitude is broken, their topographical possibilities emerge too easily. Also, their sedimented noetic context is shallow; they are thought of as games and puzzles. Our attitude to such phenomena, and thus the depth of our intentionality, is superficial. We might conclude that this phenomenology, which plays with puzzles, is merely an intellectual game, if somewhat more imaginative than most.

There is a playfulness in phenomenology, and the Husserlian emphasis upon the primacy of fantasy variations is a sign of this—but the playfulness is serious and has a purpose: eliciting structures or invariants. Ultimately, phenomenology claims that its method alone provides the adequacy needed for an ontology. But this raises a second difficulty. How is one to move from simple and abstract phenomena to more complex and "real" phenomena? And what does one discover in the process?

Here I propose another Husserlian strategy, the use of approximation. If I assume that a groundwork has been laid in the previous simple phenomenology and extrapolate the method used to more and more difficult phenomena, the trajectory of the extrapolation should become clear. Of course it is not possible in the confines of a short introduction to do anything like a step-by-step analysis, but the following description shows the scheme of investigation.

The approximations I propose are (a) a phenomenology of material objects in the visual dimension, along the same lines as those noted in the line drawings; (b) a more complex aesthetic view of objects in the natural world, which suggests the lines of variant possibilities for constituting "worlds"; (c) alternative forms of vision in aesthetic traditions as an example of visual variants; and (d) a wider and deeper cultural variant, multi-lingual ability, which, I claim, exhibits isomorphism with the previous visual variants. All but the last of the approximations are visual and so the approximations fall short of a full existential phenomenology. I make a brief note of essential phenomenological elements in each approximation so the extrapolation suggests how and why most phenomenology eventually becomes an existential phenomenology.

First, material objects: Philosophers have not only been intrigued by ambiguous appearances; they have also spent great amounts of time and ink on the ordinary furniture of the world. Keeping to the visual, and with a deliberate approximation to the conditions surrounding multi-stable figures, it is possible to project perceptual variations into the realm of material objects.

Multiple perceptual possibilities for material objects have, in fact, been noted before. Illusions in the material world are not unknown and have been part of epistemology for centuries, but it is more important to this investigation to note that many standard psychologies are aware of reversal effects in material objects.

For instance, Ernst Mach, discovered a depth reversal for a folded card viewed from above and from the front.[1] It can be seen as lying upon the table or it can be seen as standing on end. In principle this effect is isomorphic with the reversals previously noted. I shall leave it to the reader to discover whether further perceptual possibilities show themselves.

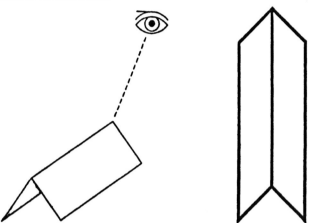

A similar effect is obtainable in a room the corners of which (preferably wall-ceiling corners of a plain-colored room) extend far enough out without connecting with other items. The point at which walls and ceiling intersect, normally seen as directed away from the viewer, can in reversed form be seen as directed towards the viewer.

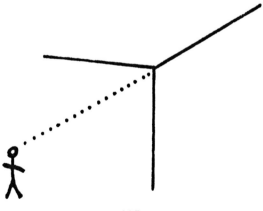

Examples can be multiplied and expanded along the lines of the previous investigation. Thus, multi-stable effects can and do occur with material objects. But in these cases there remains a certain oddness. First, such reversals and multiplications may be harder to obtain than for two-dimensional drawings. Second, the reversals are often harder to stabilize for long. Third, the object is believed not really reversed. Here there is a clue to a sediment deeper than that which displayed itself in the abstract drawings. In contrast to reversals in the drawings, repeated successes in reversal do not easily upset the privilege of one core variation.

If our examination of these reversible material objects is more closely scrutinized, several things come to attention. In both cases there is a remarkable similarity with the abstractness of the previous line drawings. Both are composed of plain surfaces uncomplicated by other configurations. Also, the viewer was directed to expect and ignore what is ordinarily seen, a type of viewing that is quasi-abstract, though directed at material objects. I shall contrast this type of seeing with what I call mundane seeing.

Mundane seeing is the involved, practical vision that characterizes most of our daily traffic with things around us. In the noetic context of mundane seeing, things are mostly use-objects or items of the environment. They are, moreover, charged with significance and not neutral, though they may be of little interest at any given moment. Some things may appear as threatening; others as beneficial and desirable; others as worth little note. Mundane vision is involved in a practical way with the surrounding environment, and the significance of what is seen occurs in that noetic context.

Abstract (including quasi-abstract) seeing sets aside the practicality of the mundane realm. It is directed to a specific theoretical concern. And that is its strength and its weakness—strength, in that, properly developed and trained, it discovers the previously unseen, weakness in that it can overlook the depth and implication of the involvement in mundane seeing.

Phenomenologically interpreted, abstract and mundane seeing are fundamentally isomorphic. They are both intentional in the deepest sense of the word, both are directed toward the surrounding world, and both have specific shapes reflexively derivable through phenomenological analysis.

Mundane and abstract seeing show two related shapes of intentionality. Both shapes are set in a full noetic context of beliefs, habits, ways of relating to phenomena—a sediment of ordered perceptual possibilities. Yet the simplified examples used for abstract seeing point up the difference between this and the more complicated and involved mundane seeing, and lead to the suspicion that whatever sediments are present in mundane seeing must be far more recalcitrant and binding for the viewer than those found in abstract seeing. This insight is the origin of the existential turn taken by most post-Husserlian phenomenology.

Existential phenomenology discovers and deepens the sense of intentionality by recognizing that even simple acts of viewing contain a latent stratum of praxical activity that ultimately implicate the very existence of the viewer. This latent stratum becomes reflexively more obvious if one imagines a variation upon mundane seeing. Suppose one sees a chair—there is a well-known illusion whereby parts of a chair are hung by nearly invisble strings, so that seen from the proper angle, the arrangement appears to be a standard chair, but from every other angle, it is seen to be a series of separate parts—which turn out not to be what it appeared to be. So long as this is a psychological experiment or an aesthetic trick, my involvement with the chair is minimal. But if I am to sit on the chair in an act that commits my body, it is much more important that the chair be what it appears to be. The very nature of abstract and quasi-abstract seeing makes this praxical element in mundane vision recede.

Existential phenomenology, with its emphasis on embodied or incarnate being (Merleau-Ponty) or being-in-the-world (Heidegger), takes this praxis stratum as basic. For existential phenomenology, seeing is seeing with one's whole body, because ultimately I commit my body through my mundane seeing. An existential turn does not deny the essential Husserlian discovery of the referentiality (directedness) of intentionality; rather it recognizes that underlying the conscious and epistemological activity of seeing, there is a total directness towards the world on the part of the human knower.

The contrast between the disengaged, but still directed and referential seeing, and the engaged, mundane seeing, illustrates that the noematic and noetic constituents are more important, and hence more "real" in the domain that calls forth action, than in an act of abstract seeing. It is tempting to conclude that this is an index to phenomenological reality. For example, in the three-dimensional reversal of a material object, the "false" appearance seems to be a fringe possibility, and the "true" appearance, the core possibility. Thus, a hierarchy of appearances can emerge, which is not so for the abstract possibilities of the line drawings.

However, a rigorous application of the phenomenological reductions precludes too easy or too early a conclusion on this matter, and the question arises whether a hierarchy correlated to praxical intentionality is the final word. Is praxical intentionality in mundane seeing analogous to the seeming naturalness of empirical order in the line drawings? And, if so, will it, too, relax its hold?

A fascinating aesthetic view of the world can be found in a further-reaching set of examples. Carlos Castaneda describes one such difficult, but captivating example in the teachings Don Juan offers him. The old wizard advises Carlos to go out and look at a tree, and instead of seeing it in the usual way (the natural attitude), he instructs him to look at the shadows, so that eventually, it is the shadows that he sees as primary. The wizard is trying to get Carlos to reverse the dominant and foreground and the recessive and background, so that the ordinary tree/shadow appearance becomes a shadow/tree appearance, a shocking reversal.

I have tried this experiment and, with difficulty, succeeded in reconstituting the tree in this way. The effect is dramatic and startling. Here a living tree in natural surroundings suddenly shows a different and radically reversed perceptual possibility. (The experiment is interesting in itself, apart from the arguments surrounding Castaneda's work.) As might be expected, breaking the usual way of seeing is much more difficult in this case than in the case of the simple multi-stable figures. Yet, once accomplished, its impact and possible implications are much more important. While I am in no way interested in becoming a wizard, the possibility of a reconstituted "world" is, at the least, intriguing.

We can point to aesthetic shifts that have actualized perceptual possibilities in the history of several cultures. One such paradigm shift, revolutionary in its day, was made by the Impressionist painters of the late nineteenth century. To simplify, it might be said that one thing the Impressionists did was to look at light instead of at objects. Claude Monet's series of cathedral paintings, made at different times of the day, illustrate this point; the object in the paintings is the effect of different light on the cathedral, each painting revealing a different possibility of lighting. This shift in both noematic and noetic context was so radical in its time, that the first viewers were said to be unable to identify the objects in the paintings.

A somewhat more radical shift occurs in a type of traditional Japanese art. In this art some object—a sparrow with a few blades of grass or a single cherry branch with blossoms—stands out against a blank or pastel background.

Our traditional way of viewing would say that the subject matter—what stands out and is dominant and in the foreground—is the sparrow or the blossoming branch. The background is merely empty or blank. This is entirely different from Western tradition in which the background is filled in. Yet the emptiness and openness of a Japanese painting *is* the subject matter of the painting, the sparrow or the branch being set there to make the openness stand out. In this, there is a radical reversal: the foreground is not dominant, the background is not recessive. To understand such a painting calls for a deep reversal in the noetic context.

It is not accidental that a similar understanding of the heavens pervades Japanese culture. In the early cosmologies of the West, the sky was the dome of the heavens, and seen as solid, its color was the color of the dome. In the East, the sky is the open and color recedes infinitely within the openness.

Although the cases mentioned above lack a full working out of a range of possibilities, they suggest what can be done and what can be expected through the extrapolation of phenomenological method. They follow a graded order, from the simplest and shallowest visual phenomena, to more complex and deeper ones. Most thoroughly worked out, abstract seeing was examined through line drawings of multi-stable objects. One step up, quasi-abstract seeing (in a restricted and isolated context) points out reversal effects in material objects. A further step up brought us to more complex, but still isolated, phenomena of the aesthetic order, which show how radical possibilities can be seen through artistic consciousness.

In each of these graded approximations of visual phenomena, the intentional phases can be noted. What is seen, the noema, is correlated to the act by which it is seen, the noesis. The noema occurs inside its field and only in relation to its field situated in its noematic context. Beliefs, expectations and habits form the correlative noetic context. The series of approximations suggest that the more complex the thing viewed, the more difficult it is to break ordinary habits of viewing, the more recalcitrant the sediments. In short, the closer one comes to mundane, praxical seeing, the more difficult it is to achieve variability, which is the field for phenomenological investigation. Yet the same essential structure of intentionality pervades each level of involvement.

In these first approximations to existential phenomenology, as in the first moves of Husserlian phenomenology, what is learned about the existent or embodied being is learned *reflexively*. The involvements I have with material objects are "read from" the objects in their relation to me. Thus while the abstract seeing of perceptual possibilities in multi-stable drawings is distant from deeper and fuller involvements, it nevertheless shows the general shape of involvement with objects. And the less demanding recalcitrance of the natural, empirical order of appearances, points to our deeper and much more recalcitrant world-beliefs and habits. Existential phenomenology takes these deeply held beliefs as its theme and examines the hold the world has on us and the hold we have on the world.

Projection: Expanding Phenomenology

Graded levels of involvement suggest that all phenomena can show variational possibilities, and until these are uncovered, phenomenology cannot operate properly. But the deeper and more complex the phenomenon and the closer to the mundane it is, the harder it is to break with the natural attitude and see the variations. This is necessarily the case: the most familiar praxical activity has the most solidly packed and total sedimentation. This sedimentation constitutes a total cultural view, which is learned and lived from childhood on.

Perhaps the closest analogue to a total cultural view occurs in learning languages. A person who is reared hearing and learning a single language and later learns a second language, usually acquires that language slowly and painfully; he does not become fluent in it, and after a certain age, cannot learn it without a permanent foreign accent.

The stages of learning the language, too, are analogous to acquiring a genuine cultural variant. At first, one gropes, with insights coming in pieces and flashes. Often one must deliberately construct a sentence and mentally translate it to, and from, the primary language. Only after a long time does the second language come easily. Although learning a second language is slower and more difficult, it, too, parallels the process of gaining variations in multi-stable phenomena. One does not lose the apodicticity of the primary language, but it is seen to be but one way of "saying the world."

Another analogy with multi-stable phenomena is that once a second language is learned, subsequent languages come more and more easily. A further parallel occurs in that the different ways of "saying the world" in the second and third language seem dramatic and striking, but once the acquisition of language possibilities becomes familiar, this drama recedes and is replaced by a deeper understanding of the essential structure of "saying the world." Languages, in this sense, are profound ways of seeing the world.[2]

However, the language analogue is a much more comprehensive and complex phenomenon than the line-drawing examples worked out here. The infinite, yet structured, possibilities of natural languages are such, that a language may be a total view; the pervasiveness of language is such that its particular perspective is deeply engrained culturally and usually remains sedimented throughout one's life. Here, to my mind, is an essential reason why languages ought to be required for all higher education. To loosen the grip of the single view is a prerequisite for appreciation of varying views of the world.

The language example also makes the perspectival relativity implicit in variational theory apparent in a somewhat elevated way. Natural languages may, indeed, be considered the perspectives on the world of the people who speak them. I do not here wish to enter into the debate about whether a language determines the entire way in which we view the world (Whorf) or whether languages are so distinctive that radical translation is in fact impossible (Quine); but if one assumes there are internal focuses in language that help make the language distinctive, one can discern essential features of a linguistic perspective. To attain the essential features of a linguistic perspective, phenomenology would have to find the adequate variations. Of course, this would be no small task to complete for a series of languages.

Take a simple instance of existential-cultural relativity. That Eskimos have many words for snow; that the Arab languages have many words for camel; and that American English does not, is a well-worn point by now. A similar example emerges from recent history—American English is adept at creating new terms for technological artifacts, a tendency deplored by those who govern the French Academy. The result is that technological terms from American English now pervade French, both the technologists' tribal language and everyday speech. With technology goes language.

Clearly, multiplicity obtains if and when there are serious existential and cultural relations with an object. Skiers, who find it necessary to make more than the ordinary observation about snow, have caused some distinctions to be made (even in American English) for snow: "corn," "powder," "iced." Essentially languages can say what needs to be said, but the way in which they say it will vary widely and be related to a "form of life."

Projection: Expanding Phenomenology

The relativities in these illustrations are commonplace, but the phenomenological point is the experiential and essential ground for why and how such relativities take shape. What is the ground for the often noted difference in time perception among the Hopi Indians and contemporary Americans? This question does not arise unless the relativity is possible and appreciated. But once it is possible and appreciated, the range of variation and its deeper structure must be investigated. A phenomenological look at linguistic and cultural relativities goes beyond both assertion of cultural superiority (often made in extremely subtle ways in contemporary philosophies) and vacuous play among the richness of relativities.

If there is a depth structure of invariance, this is what must be sought through relativities. And this is the task of an informed phenomenology. The complexity of relativities point to yet another aspect of phenomenology in the future: to be informed, phenomenology must necessarily rely upon other disciplines. Its view of these disciplines, and particularly its interpretation of what they are doing, may be widely different from what those within the disciplines interpret their task and method to be, but without these other disciplines, phenomenology would be restricted to the realm of first-person experience. Intersubjective phenomenology is necessarily interdisciplinary phenomenology.

Notes

1. Fred Attneave, "Multistability in Perception," *Scientific American*, Dec. 1971, p. 68.

2. See Martin Heidegger, "Conversation with a Japanese" in *On the Way to Language* (New York: Harper and Row, 1971), pp. 1–54.

Chapter Nine

Interdisciplinary Phenomenology

Husserl's early and most optimistic view of the future of phenomenology was that all the sciences could and should be reconstructed along phenomenological lines. That at least some sciences could benefit from phenomenology has been indicated here in at least suggested form. For example, the empirical psychology of perception would be informed and opened to new directions by the essential science of descriptive phenomenology. Husserl held that an essential or eidetic science necessarily precedes an empirical science, and the discovery of a wider and deeper field of perceptual possibilities for multi-stable figures illustrates that there is such an essential level from which any empirical set of sediments might arise.

Once the phenomenological inversion has occurred, the wider field of possibilities is the essential one within which particular arrangements take shape. Not all fields of possibilities are arranged in the same way, as shown by a comparison between the investigation with multi-stable phenomena and the brief foray into similar occurrences with material objects. But all fields of possibilities display some type of topography, which becomes apparent only when the field itself is opened to the essential insight of the rigorously descriptive phenomenological look.

This Husserlian emphasis upon the primacy of the possible is the radical side of phenomenology and exemplifies its claim to be foundational with respect to the field of human experience. But there is another side to the issue of phenomenology and its relationship to the other disciplines. In the second half of the twentieth century, it is no longer possible for one person to acquire a large enough proportion of knowledge in every discipline, even to know what variations might be possible for a given domain of inquiry. For phenomenology to begin its investigation and critique of possibility fields, it must look to already constituted disciplines.

I have emphasized in this study the necessity of first-person experience in doing phenomenology—this is indeed the first word for phenomenology. Experiential verification is the second word, insofar as experiences reported by or taken from others must be scrutinized as possible, fulfillable experiences. But because the essential field is the entire field of possible experience, it is already in principle *intersubjective,* open to anyone willing and trained to follow the investigation.

The disciplines from which phenomenology must draw material for examination already contain latent insights and forms of variations that may be reinterpreted phenomenologically. The task is to discern what the leading problems are in relation to the framework that phenomenology, as a science of the possible, offers.

The connection of phenomenology with other disciplines is not original here. It has been pointed up particularly by the contemporary philosopher Paul Ricoeur. His "diagnostic" use of a whole span of disciplines in his own thought draws on the informative power of constituted disciplines, and his emphasis on the genuine otherness of the disciplines complements the less cautious claim of the earlier Husserl.[1]

It would be too ambitious and presumptuous, at the end of this book, to suggest a total reorganization along Husserlian lines. Moreover, to end with a system for applied phenomenology would breach the modesty fitting to a pragmatic American approach to things. But I shall note one phenomenological development in each of the main divisions of the disciplines. Where possible, I shall suggest a development in the general area of experience and its role in the sciences or arts. I am not suggesting that these developments are more basic or important than other phenomenological influences on the disciplines, only that they illustrate how one might deal with a problem in a discipline in a phenomenological way.

The Natural Sciences

From a phenomenological point of view, the natural sciences might be called noematic sciences insofar as their domains of objectivity are primarily concerned with object correlates. From their own point of view, noematic sciences may be little concerned with how a given field of inquiry relates to human intentionality. Philosophically, however, this concentration on noema can allow the correlated noetic questions to be overlooked. The question of how a given phenomenon is or may be made present, necessarily, leads in a philosophical direction. For phenomenology, the practice of science is a particular form of and development of human intentionality. Thus one important question is how the observer is and can be intentionally related to a phenomenon; in contemporary scientific contexts this can be an exceedingly complex problem.

To observe implies some type of experiencing, and this experiencing in contemporary science is a question for the investigating phenomenologist. For the moment, I shall set aside three clearly important aspects of observation in the scientific context: seeing as it occurs within a community of technical discourse (itself strikingly different from ordinary discourse), the laboratory practices that are taken for granted in that context, and the relation of observation to predictive theory as such. Each of these problems is important and has been dealt with in the philosophy of science. Instead, I shall focus on some basic perceptual elements that are part of scientific observation. There is at least one analogy between scientific experience and phenomenological understanding of experience. Both deconstruct and transform ordinary experience. The scientist implicitly knows that intuitions are constituted. What he sees may be very different from what the uninformed individual sees, and this relates to the noetic context, which is quite differently and technically developed in science. It is necessary for both science and phenomenology to be able to take apart what is given so that its deeper strata may be discovered; in this, both transform what is taken to be intuitive.

The separation of scientists from the points of view of ordinary expectations leads to a different view of things and can cause problems. Today the sciences tend increasingly to bring microphenomena into the center of interest. Particle theory and genetic theory are paradigm examples of disciplines concerned with microphenomena.

Observation of microphenomena, considered apart from the question of predictive theorizing, poses new problems for understanding what scientific observation perceives. Often scientists retain a strong sense of realism when dealing with microphenomena, but the more microscopic the observations, the harder they are to observe. Science asks whether or not there is an ultimate indivisible unit of physical reality. The companion question is whether or not there is a limit to observability. For example, particles are found by their traces; they are smashed at ultra high speeds into other entities, and the remains of these collisions are examined for traces. Here ordinary perceptions are seemingly left far behind, and science is often tempted to hypothesize, in an ancient echo of the Greek atomists, that the smallest particles not only are impossible to perceive in fact, but impossible to detect in principle. At this borderline, the realism of the inquiry itself comes under suspicion, since it becomes difficult, if not impossible, to discern the difference between a purely theoretical (or imagined) entity and an empirical one.

Observations of this kind are made by means of instruments. Indeed, the more minute the phenomena, the larger and more complex the instruments.[2] It is here that an interesting set of questions can be raised for phenomenology.

What happens to and in perception when it occurs by means of an instrument? How is the perceptual intentionality of the observer mediated, and with what result? Such questions lead to a phenomenology of instrument-mediated perceptions as important for understanding how contemporary science situates its observation and its claims for its observations.

That such observations are still perception is clear enough. The scientist observes dial readings and tracings on photographic and computer-generated plates and, at least for confirmations of his theories, relates to a world through, with, or by instruments.

One phenomenologically oriented philosopher of science, Patrick Heelan, has argued that the use of instruments modifies perception substantially. He holds that the "worlds" constituted through direct or mundane perception experience and the "world" developed through scientific instruments are different, the ordinary "world" being constituted by ordinary perceptions and the scientific "world" being constituted by instrument-embodied perceptions.[3]

I have taken note of this suggestion in a somewhat broader context and attempted to consider what occurs when experience is directed through, with, and among technological artifacts (machines), of which scientific instruments are a sub-class.[4] A few illustrations from this as yet preliminary development will point up the implications of instrument-mediated perception. In the quotations that follow, substitute "instrument" for "machine," and the point will be clear.

> I begin with certain simple experiences with machines and with the simple kinds of machines I can find. I pick up a pencil or a piece of chalk and begin to trace it across the desk or blackboard. Upon a careful examination of this experience, I suddenly discover that I experience the blackboard or the desk *through* the chalk—I *feel* the smoothness or the roughness of the board *at the end of the chalk*. This is, of course, also Merleau-Ponty's blind man who experiences the "world" at the end of his cane. If I begin to be descriptively rigorous,

I find I must say that what I feel is felt locally at the end of the chalk or, better, at the chalk-blackboard junction. The "terminus" of my intentional extension into the world is on the blackboard, and I have discovered (contrary to empiricism) that touch is also a distance sense.

If I continue the reflection in terms of the phenomenological understanding of intentionality as experience within a world, I note that there is something curious about this experience. First, I clearly do not, in the case given, primarily experience the chalk as either thematic or as an object. Rather, what I experience is the blackboard and more precisely, a certain complex aspect of the blackboard's presence as texture, hardness, resistance, etc. I discern that I experience the blackboard *through* the chalk, the chalk being taken into my "self-experiencing."

By this I mean that the chalk is only secondarily an "object," while more primarily it is absorbed into my experiencing as an extension of myself. It is true, that the chalk is not totally absorbed in that I have what might be called an "echo focus" in which I feel simultaneously a certain pressure at the juncture fingers/chalk with what I feel at the end of the chalk. Nevertheless, in the primary focus it is the board which I feel.[5]

A phenomenological interpretation of what happens in one type of machine-mediated experience is shown in the next quotation, where I follow the same general correlational interpretation of noema-noesis, here called the human-world correlation.

This phenomenon may now be explicated in terms of the correlation model I have already noted. However, it is important to note where the machine is placed within the correlation. In the first case above, it becomes clear that the proper placing of the machine here must be upon the correlation line itself:

Human-machine———▶World.

The machine is "between" me and what is experienced and is in this sense a "means" of experience in the primary focus. Here, because the chalk is not thematized, it may be spoken of as a partial symbiotic part of the noetic act or of the experiencing of the noematic correlate in the world. This may be symbolized as follows by the introduction of parentheses:

Interdisciplinary Phenomenology

(Human-machine)——▶World.

With this we have one type of human-machine relation, an experience *through* a machine. The correlational structure of intentionality remains, in that I do experience something other than the machine being used, and at the same time, my experiencing is extended through the machine for that intentional fulfillment. I may thus describe the chalk as having a partial *transparency relation* between myself and what is other. And in fact, the better the machine, the more "transparency" there is. Likewise, I can use a language now, which speaks of the machine as part of myself or taken into myself, so far as the experience is concerned.[6]

The machine- or instrument-mediated experience in which the instrument is taken into one's experience of bodily engaging the world, whether it be primarily kinesthetic-tactile or the extended embodiment of sight (telescope) or sound (telephone), I term an embodiment relation. These relations genuinely extend intentionality into the world, and when they operate properly, the sense of a new realism in the phenomenon can be retained. But this extension is not without other implications.

However, in such cases the transparency itself is enigmatic. It is clear that I do experience the board through the chalk, but it is equally clear that what is experienced is in some ways *transformed*. I do not experience the board through the chalk in the same way that I experience the board "in the flesh" with my own finger. Thus, when I compare my experience of the blackboard through the chalk and with my naked finger, I may note that in both cases I get a texture with its roughness or smoothness. But with my finger, I also get warmth or coolness, a spread sense of the spatiality of the board, perhaps also its dustiness or cleanness. There is a greater richness to the naked touch of the blackboard than the blackboard experienced through the chalk. I may now speak of the experiences of the blackboard through the chalk as a reduced experience when compared with my "naked" touch of the board.

Suppose, however, I replace the chalk with a finer instrument, let us say a dentist's probe made of stainless steel with a fine pick at the end. As I trace the probe across the board, I note more distinctly and clearly than before, each imperfection of the board's surface. Each pock mark or crack appears through my probe in an *amplified* way;

141

perhaps even what I neither saw nor felt with even my naked finger becomes present through the steel probe. A microscopic presence is amplified through the probe, thus extending my experience of the board to a level of discernment previously unnoted.

In each of these variations in the experienced use of machines, I continue to note that the embodiment relation is one in which I do experience otherness through the machine, but that the experience through the machine transforms or stands in contrast to my ordinary experience in the "flesh."[7]

However, instrumentation that embodies perception is not the only instrumental possibility for perception. At a quite different pole of the correlational continuum a different possibility may be noted.

Suppose I investigate the basements of a modern university and I come upon a room filled with dials, gauges, rheostats and switches watched intently by a heating engineer. Suppose this control center monitors all the heating and cooling systems of the offices and dormitories. The engineer in the case "reads" his dials and if one creeps up, indicating that Quad X is overheating, he merely has to turn a dial and watch to see if the heat begins to turn to normal. If it does, all right, if not, he may have to call a building manager to find out what has broken down. Here the engineer is engaged in experiences *of* a machine.

Returning to our correlational model, this experience of a machine is curious. Through the machine something (presumably) still happens elsewhere, only in this case the engineer does not experience the terminus of the intention which traverses the machine. Thus we may model the relation as follows:

Human⟶(machine-World).

His primary experiential terminus is with the machine. I shall thus call this relation a *hermeneutic relation*. There is a partial opacity between the machine and the world and thus the machine is something like a text. I may read an author, but the author is only indirectly present in the text. It is precisely in such situations that Kafkaesque possibilities may arise (imagine that the heat dial has gone awry and in fact, when the engineer thinks the heat is going down, it is actually going up—or better, simply imagine registrars who relate more immediately on a daily basis to computers than to students). Of course, in these instances there is still a possibility of employing the difference between mediated and unmediated types of experience; the engineer could go to the dorm himself to note what was happening.

In some cases instruments probe into areas previously unknown where such checking is not at all possible, and in this case, we have a genuine hermeneutic situation in which it is the hermeneut who enters the cavern to hear the saying of the oracle and we are left to his interpretation. Thus, those instruments which probe the ultramicroscopic worlds of the atom leave room for doubt as to what precisely is "on the other side" of the machine.[8]

While this is very schematic, it points up an area in which a phenomenology of perception is relevant to an increasingly important problem in the investigation of microphenomena. Such a phenomenology ultimately ought to be able to outline the conditions of the possibilities of instrument-mediated observation and its attendant problems. But to do so in detail requires being informed by practicing the science itself. It is also a phenomenology that elevates a philosophy of technology to the level of importance now occupied by the philosophy of science, with its focus on the concept of theory.

The Social Sciences

If concentration on otherness in the noematic field leads to calling the natural sciences noematic sciences, social sciences might be termed noetic sciences, the reason being that the social sciences, notably sociology and anthropology but also history and some versions of psychology, concentrate on the field of constituted human meanings. The social, or human sciences turn to questions, in a phenomenological sense, which can be called questions about the origin, development, structure and sedimentation of belief contexts as they impinge on human action.

Phenomenological work in the social sciences is probably better known and more thoroughly developed than in the natural sciences, and so there are a number of well-known phenomenologically informed sources. An early standard work was that of Alfred Schutz (see his *Collected Papers* and *Philosophy of the Social Sciences* edited by Maurice Natanson), and a very recent phenomenologically oriented development has been the rise of ethnomethodology, led by Harold Garfinkel.

Between these two well-known phenomenological developments in the social sciences stands the work of Peter Berger and Thomas Luckmann, who have taken up the task of a phenomenological development of sociology and the sociology of knowledge. I shall briefly point out a few elements in their *The Social Construction of Reality* to illustrate how phenomenology operates as a noetic science in the social sciences.

Once the basic language and conceptual system of phenomenology is grasped, it is quite easy to make the transition to the technical language employed by Berger and Luckmann (more closely derived from Husserl and Schutz than the language used in this book). They, too, hold that philosophical, pre-sociological considerations must be attended to before sociology can begin. "The method we consider best suited to clarify the foundations of knowledge in everyday life is that of phenomenological analysis, a purely descriptive method and, as such, 'empirical' but not 'scientific'—as we understand the nature of the empirical sciences."[9]

They consider the primary preliminary task of the social sciences to be the understanding of what and how the world of everyday life is constituted. In short, the descriptive task is an analysis of what is already sedimented and taken for granted, a phenomenology of the natural attitude.

Among the multiple realities there is one that presents itself as the reality par excellence. This is the reality of everyday life. Its privileged position entitles it to the designation of paramount reality. The tension of consciousness is highest in everyday life, that is, the latter imposes itself upon consciousness in the most massive, urgent and intense manner. It is impossible to ignore, difficult even to weaken in its imperative presence. . . . This wide-awake state of existing in and apprehending the reality of everyday life is taken by me to be normal and self-evident, that is, it constitutes my natural attitude.[10]

What is here examined is the rise, structure and constitution of a meaning-structure, the socially noetic state of everyday life.

Once the region of investigation is cleared, the description proceeds in typical phenomenological fashion. The range of experience in everyday life is seen to display itself in terms of a series of zones, which clearly approximate the focus-field-horizon structure elaborated previously in the multi-stable examples.

> The reality of everyday life is organized around the "here" of my body and the "now" of my present focus. This "here and now" is the focus of my attention to the reality of everyday life. What is "here and now" presented to me in everyday life is the *realissimum* of my consciousness. The reality of everyday life is not, however, exhausted by these immediate presences, but embraces phenomena that are not present "here and now." This means that I experience everyday life in terms of differing degrees of closeness and remoteness, both spatially and temporally. Closest to me is the zone of everyday life that is directly accessible to my bodily manipulation. . . . I know, of course, that the reality of everyday life contains zones that are not accessible to me in this manner. But either I have no pragmatic interest in these zones or my interest in the far zones is less intense and certainly a less urgent field-fringe.[11]

Further, in a social noetic interest, a phenomenological sociology takes note of the intersubjective nature of the structures of everyday life. "The reality of everyday life further presents itself to me as an intersubjective world, a world that I share with others. This intersubjectivity sharply differentiates everyday life from other realities of which I am conscious."[12] Here the field of interest narrows to noetic, intersubjective phenomena and the isolation of the stratum of social meanings, the second of which has become the subject matter for phenomenological sociology. "Most importantly, I know that there is an ongoing correspondence between *my* meanings and *their* meanings in this world, that we share a common sense about its reality. The natural attitude is the attitude of commonsense consciousness precisely because it refers to a world that is common to many men."[13]

EXPERIMENTAL PHENOMENOLOGY

The problem for investigation, then, becomes the structure of reality of this natural attitude, of everyday life in its intersubjective constitution. Sedimentation occurs in the intersubjective noetic structure, and the processes of sedimentation are looked at phenomenologically. Berger and Luckmann see this process largely as occurring through tradition and through what they (following Schutz) term objectivation. Objectivation is the process of experience moving into language, which in turn is a social bond and institution of intersubjective meanings. Sedimentation and tradition, then, are the background against which empirical everyday life occurs.

What appears here is a new horizon structure (origins: real, constructed, lost, etc.) which limits the possibilities of a field:

> Only a small part of the totality of human experiences is retained in consciousness. The experiences that are so retained become sedimented, that is, they congeal in recollection as recognizable and memorable entities. Unless such sedimentation took place, the individual could not make sense of his biography.[14]

Phenomenological sociology sees sedimentation as having an (immediate) experiential origin and being the genesis of objectivated meanings (taken-for-granted beliefs). Berger and Luckmann give the following simple example:

> For example, only some members of a hunting society have the experience of losing their weapons and being forced to fight a wild animal with their bare hands. This frightening experience with whatever lessons in bravery, cunning and skill it yields, is firmly sedimented in the consciousness of the individuals who went through it. If the experience is shared by several individuals, it will be sedimented intersubjectively, may perhaps even form a bond between those individuals.[15]

This primary experience, shared by a few, can, however, be objectivated as a possible experience.

> As this experience is designated and transmitted linguistically, however, it becomes accessible and, perhaps, strongly relevant to in-

dividuals who have never gone through it. The linguistic designation . . . abstracts the experience from its individual biographical occurrences. It becomes an objective possibility for everyone, or at any rate for everyone within a certain type. . . ; that is, it becomes anonymous in principle, even if it is still associated with the feats of specific individuals.[16]

In this way objectivation leads to institution, ritualization and the sedimentation of social possibilities.

Berger and Luckmann see this process happening primarily through language, which is the bearer of social sedimentation. "Language becomes the depository of a large aggregate of collective sedimentations, which can be acquired monothetically, that is, as cohesive wholes and without reconstructing their original process of formation."[17] When this happens, social sediment becomes an accepted, taken-for-granted belief which can lose or vary its justification. It becomes a static structure, a given, within social reality.

I shall not trace this analysis further other than to say that, seen as a noetic structure, the phenomenology of everyday life and its sediments can go on to deal with such aspects of sedimentation as the necessary simplifications that allow sediment to be easily transmitted typifications, the way in which sedimentation becomes abstracted and ritualized, how it becomes equated with (social) knowledge, and is passed on from person to person.

Anthropological studies show many and various empirical constructions in human societies, and even variants within societies. What is of interest to a noetic science is the nature of the structure of sedimentation and tradition that produces these variants.

The Arts

The third set of disciplines to which an interdisciplinary phenomenology must relate are the arts, both literary and fine. Functioning as it does from a base of possibility fields, phenomenology is sure to find the arts a rich source, since they stimulate much creative imagination. The arts, taken as disciplines in which possibilities are explored and displayed for whatever motives (art for its own sake or for other purposes), practice possibility exploration and so have a profound relation to a central element and need of phenomenology. There is a deep relationship between artistic possibility exploration and possibility exploration in phenomenology which reveals the kinship between phenomenology and art. A phenomenological aesthetics, on which there has been some work, would surely view the arts as exercises in variations. The visual arts, for example, seek to explore the field of visual possibilities; music explores the auditory dimension; sculpture and architecture explore the spatial and material; and dance (and some sports) explores the field of bodily motion.

While not lacking noematic and noetic aspects, the arts, unlike the noematic and noetic sciences, exercise intentionality itself *as* variational. There is a playfulness in art deeply related to phenomenological playfulness, and it is possible to see the practice of the artist as latently phenomenological from the outset.

In actually exercising fantasy variations, the arts echo the Aristotelean dictum that poetics is ultimately more true than history. It is out of possibility that the undiscovered is found and created.

Given this relationship between phenomenology and art, it is no accident that almost every phenomenologist (at least since Husserl) has made some comment on the arts or made a more systematic foray into examining them. Martin Heidegger has examined poetry (*Existence and Being*, for example); Jean-Paul Sartre, numerous literary topics *(Situations)*, Maurice Merleau-Ponty, visual art *(Signs and Sense and Nonsense)*, and many others.

There have also been attempts to develop a phenomenological aesthetics and literary theory. Roman Ingarden's *The Literary Work of Art* and Mikel Dufrenne's *Phenomenology of Aesthetic Experience* stand out.

But to comment on phenomenology and art at a more basic level, the level at which the variational richness of art emerges, is to look at the activity of imagination. Imagination has been a theme of many phenomenologists, but one of the most systematic works has just appeared, *Imagining: A Phenomenological Study* by Edward S. Casey.

A phenomenology of imagination spans all the arts and isolates an essential intentional dimension in disciplines that strive for a display of possibilities. Casey's analysis is cognizant of this aim and its profound relationship to phenomenology. His thesis, which emerges from a concrete, descriptive study of the imagination, is that the imagination is uniquely autonomous, though initially he characterizes this autonomy as thin.

> Recognizing the thin character of imaginative autonomy vis-à-vis other denser types of autonomy may help us to understand why the autonomous action of imagining has so often been questioned—or simply bypassed—by previous investigators. It is as if they had asked themselves the following skeptical question: How can an experience so tenuous, so fragile and fleeting as imagining be autonomous? Overlooked in this question is the possibility that imagining's very tenuousness may provide a clue to its mode of autonomy. Perhaps imagining is autonomous *in its very insubstantiality.*

> But what then *is* imaginative autonomy? The answer to this question may be encapsulated in the following two statements:
> 1. The autonomy of imagining consists in its strict independence from other mental acts, from its surroundings, and from all pressing human concerns.
> 2. The autonomy of imagining consists in the freedom of mind of which imagination is uniquely capable.[18]

This phenomenology of imagination shows, in contrast to many previous theories, that the role of imagination is an irreducible function of intentionality. Its autonomy, the autonomy of the multiplicity of intentional acts, is one irreducible role of mind.

> . . . A recognition of the multiplicity of the mental—a multiplicity that is borne out precisely by the existence of eidetic differences between various kinds of mental acts—must replace a vertical view of mind if we are to avoid the harmful consequences of thinking in ex-

clusively hierarchical terms. It is only within the mind's multiplex structure that imagination's autonomy has its place—a place which, however singular it may be, is not rankable as topmost, *or* as bottom-most, *or* as middlemost.[19]

This seems like a modest claim for imagination. It is thin and but one of a group of mental activities. Moreover, Casey argues that the imagination per se is not necessarily creative in either the artistic or unartistic sense. "*[T]here is no inherent or necessary connection between imagining and being creative; they are only contingently connected.*"[20] However, according to Casey, the thin autonomy of the imagination has a unique role. It is the intentional activity that opens the field of pure possibility.

Pure possibility, finally, is the thetic expression of imaginative freedom of mind. Even if the purely possible is subject to certain formal and practical limits, these ultimate boundaries are not nearly so constrictive as those imposed upon whatever is empirically real. Pure possibility enables the mind's free movement to traverse a terrain considerably more vast than the region occupied by perceived and remembered things alone. . . . Each journey into such a domain is potentially endless, since a given series of pure possibilities has no fixed terminus. Here freedom is the freedom of never having to come to a pre-established or peremptory end.[21]

Possibility as such arises from imagination, Casey claims, because it is the nature of imagination to vary itself. Variations are the very life of imagination.

. . . In the present context such multiplicity assumes the specific form of *variability*, that is, the mind's freedom to vary itself indefinitely and without end. . . .

Variation means multiplicity; being a variation upon something else, a given variation always implies *other* variations, actual or possible. Consequently, a mental act whose basic operations continually engender variety will be free in the special sense of giving rise to multiple options, directions and routes.[22]

150

Thus in spite of his very moderate claims for imagination, admitting its thinness, its lack of either inferiority or superiority over other mental (intentional) dimensions, Casey ends up seeing in imagining a link to human freedom.

> To be free in this fashion is to realize freedom of mind to the fullest. For the human mind thrives on variation, even as it seeks unification; and imagining, more than any other mental act, proceeds by proliferation: it is the primary way in which the mind diversifies itself and its contents. Mind is free—is indeed most free—in imagining.[23]

Without detracting from Casey's conclusions, I take exception to locating freedom solely in the imagination. Multi–stable phenomena as well have opened the way for finding variations and possibilities within perception. Accepting the recalcitrance of variations in perception, linked as perception is to the basic praxis of bodily life (in contrast to the floating freedom of the imagination), it remains the case that every dimension of intentionality displays a possibility field.

However, imagination, with its freedom to dissociate, to place imagining far from mundane concerns in its own natural *epoché*, brings variability directly and immediately to the fore. Most prosaically, infinite variability of imagining may be seen in its spontaneity and its capacity to be continued indefinitely without regard to constraints. "Just as we are only rarely coerced to imagine in the first place, so we are almost never obliged to proceed in accordance with what we have already imagined."[24]

It has already been noted how essential the capacity to vary things is to phenomenological philosophy. Casey sees the same capacity as essential to the arts.

> The possibilizing activity of imagination in art opens up an experiential domain which would not otherwise have been available, either to the artist or the spectator. This domain is one in which *everything appears as purely possible.* Within the medium bound, spatio-tempor-

al limits of a given work of art, the domain of the purely possible emerges whenever imagining is functioning autonomously.[25]

The realm of the possible, opened by imaginative variations, is the common ground of the arts and phenomenology—each according to its respective purpose.

> . . . It is imagining *as autonomous* which introduces the factor of pure possibility into aesthetic experience. Only an autonomous imagination can project, explore and populate the domain of the purely possible in art. This domain is intrinsic to the very being of works of art, and yet it is left unaccounted for in representationalist and expressivist theories, both of which fail to appreciate the autonomous activity of imagination in artistic creation and enjoyment. . . . In art—whether in making or contemplating it—we not only perceive or feel; we also imagine, thereby entering a realm that would otherwise have remained closed to us.[26]

Multiplicity, variation, pure possibility: this is the region in which a healthy art and a rigorous phenomenology can and must play. Whether this region is thin, as Casey holds, or the ultimate source of discovery of both the real and the irreal, as Husserl held, phenomenology and art are kin.

Yet the genius of phenomenology, which makes it so different from its nearest of kin, binds its playfulness to a desire to create new sciences. Only through variation, Husserl claims, does the invariant show itself; only through phenomenology is a fundamental ontology possible, claims Heidegger. Neither of these claims concerns the arts; but they are essential to phenomenology. But this is merely to say that art is not philosophy, and philosophy is not art, even though an artful philosophy is to be preferred to any other kind.

Epilogue

Art, science and philosophy are activities performed by practitioners in communities of discourse. In philosophy the community of discourse is diverse, and not all practitioners understand each others' dialects, nor are the various dances that philosophers perform with mind and mouth the same. It has always been thus, and likely will continue to be so, since philosophies are also variants, though spelled very large. I have tried here to show a few steps in the dance that is phenomenology, but only some elementary ones. I hope there are those who can do the same steps and find in them an excitement and satisfaction that will lead further. To phenomenology there is no end.

Notes

1. Paul Ricoeur's "diagnostics" develop this interdisciplinary approach characteristic of all his work. See especially *Freedom and Nature* (Evanston: Northwestern University Press, 1966), pp. 13-17.

2. Kosta Gavroglu, a research physicist, believes that this is not an accidental trait in seeking microphenomena, but that larger and larger instrumentation will be called for.

3. Patrick Heelan, "Horizon, Objectivity and Reality in the Physical Sciences," *International Philosophical Quarterly*, Vol. VII, 1967, pp. 375-412.

4. Don Ihde, "The Experience of Technology," *Cultural Hermeneutics*, Vol. 2, 1974, pp. 267-279.

5. Ibid., p. 271.

6. Ibid., p. 272.

7. Ibid., pp. 272-3.

8. Ibid., pp. 275-6.

9. Peter L. Berger and Thomas Luckmann, *The Social Construction of Reality* (New York: Doubleday and Co., 1966), p. 20.

10. Ibid., p. 21.

11. Ibid., p. 22.

12. Ibid., p. 22.

13. Ibid., p. 23.

14. Ibid., p. 63.

15. Ibid., p. 64.

16. Ibid., p. 65.

17. Ibid., p. 66.

18. Edward S. Casey, *Imagining: A Phenomenological Study* (Bloomington: Indiana University Press, 1976), p. 191.

19. Ibid., p. 178.

20. Ibid., p. 188.

21. Ibid., p. 199.

22. Ibid., p. 200.

23. Ibid., pp. 200-1.

24. Ibid., pp. 179-180.

25. Ibid., p. 206.

26. Ibid., p. 207.

Index of Names

Aristotle, 31, 38
Attneave, Fred, 108n, 133n
Berger, Peter, 144, 146–147
Bruno, Giordano 19
Casey, Edward S. 149–152
Castaneda, Carlos, 128
Copernicus, Nicolas, 18–19, 31
Da Vinci, Leonardo, 68
Descartes, Rene, 53
Dufrenne, Mikel, 148
Garfinkel, Harold, 144
Gavroglu, Kosta, 153n
Heelan, Patrick, 139
Hegel, G. W. F. 51
Heidegger, Martin 14–15, 17, 26n, 29, 89, 127, 148, 152
Husserl, Edmund, 14–15, 17, 21–22, 26n, 29, 33, 38, 41–46, 63, 73, 89, 135
Ingarten, Roman, 148

James, William, 55
Kant, Immanuel 20, 41
Kierkegaard, Soren, 51
Kuhn, Thomas, 18
Luckmann, Thomas 144, 146–147
Mach, Ernst, 124
Merleau-Ponty, Maurice, 14, 20, 26n, 47, 127, 139, 148
Michelangelo, 68
Monet, Claude, 129
Natanson, Maurice, 144
Necker, Louis, 118
Nietzsche, Friedrich, 20
Plato, 88
Quine, Willard van Orman, 132
Ricoeur, Paul, 89, 136, 153n
Sartre, Jean Paul, 148
Schutz, Alfred, 143–144
Whorf, Benjaman, 132

Printed in the United States
41110LVS00006B/262-291